MW00573271

Praise for *Divine Mother, D*

"Donna D'Ingillo's book is a gift to all of creation. She shows us how to have a deep personal relationship with our spiritual parents. As you read the words of this profound book you begin to fall in love with your spirit Mother and Father. Thank you Donna for this life-changing book!"
—Sharon Lanier

"This fabulous compilation from the Creators of our universe offer an incredible opportunity to reach deeper into our spiritual lives."
—James Lease, artist, illustrator, urban designer

"I sat right next to Donna for years as she transmitted our divine parents, and I can verify her devotion to the truth of this process. I can attest to the clarity of what comes through her that so deeply impressed our group at the time. We often left these sessions in tears of joy and laughter. Thank you, Donna, for all those unforgettable times, and for your new transmissions in this book."
—Jerry Lane, author of *The Adventure of Being Human* series; former U.S. Marine platoon commander

"This is truly a work of deep devotion to assist our human family in understanding the reality of who we are as spirit beings and the depth of love that is available to us. This compilation of messages draws the reader into a realm of connection with our divinity unlike the traditional scriptures that endeavor to trap us in religious dogma and division. These messages will grow on everyone but at a different pace, as the reader is ready."
—Yvonne Williams, artist and author of *Slaves of a Different Kind*

"This book is to be read and re-read by anyone with a deep desire to open to the love, peace, and goodness within."
—Laura Maher, author of *Auntie Mom*

"*Divine Mother, Divine Father* is a lovely, gentle book full of meditations for personal spiritual growth. I think anyone reading this will be touched by the love that shines throughout."
—Virginia Brooks

Divine Mother, Divine Father

Divine Mother, Divine Father

Teachings on Inspired Living from Our Heavenly Parents

Donna D'Ingillo

Origin Press

Also from Our Celestia Imprint:

The Center Within: *Lessons from the
Heart of the Urantia Revelation* (1998)

Teach Us to Love: *Finding Unconditional
Love through Communion with God* (2011)

The Adventure of Being Human I: *Lessons on Soulful
Living from the Heart of the Urantia Revelation* (2012)

The Adventure of Being Human II: *Mother Spirit Speaks* (2015)

Origin Press

PO Box 151117
San Rafael, CA 94915
www.OriginPress.org

ISBN: 978-1-57983-047-2

Printed in the United States of America

First printing: November 2016

This book is dedicated to truth-seekers and light-bringers
all around the planet for your efforts to uplift humanity
to the ways of Spirit. May you be abundantly
blessed for your sacred work.

Acknowledgments

Many thanks to my editor and publisher Byron Belitsos for polishing this book to make it sparkle, to Elianne Obadia for her help and encouragement during the early stages of the book's development, and to Albert Haldane and Simha Serayar their excellent proofing.

I am deeply grateful to my partner Daniel Jones for his support of my life's work, and to all of the people who have supported the ministry of the Center for Christ Consciousness over the years.

I thank my Divine Mother and Father for their love and validation of who I am, and for the many celestial helpers who have encouraged and supported me through many trials and challenges of life.

A Note to the Reader on Terminology

Because *Divine Mother, Divine Father* is closely linked to *The Urantia Book*, it contains some unfamiliar terms. First published in 1955, the Urantia Revelation offers a new philosophy, cosmology, history, and theology for our times. In particular, Jesus Christ is designated with a unique phraseology. In the lengthy biography of Jesus supplied in the Urantia text—and elsewhere in the book—he is depicted with titles and names unknown in the Christian tradition, such as *Christ Michael* and *Michael*. In another break with the past, he is also described as having a co-equal deity consort known as *Mother Spirit* or *Divine Mother*, who bears many of the same divine traits as the figures of Mary or Sophia from the Christian tradition, or the idea of the Holy Spirit. This is a unique theology, and it is best understood in the context of the new cosmology presented in the Urantia Revelation, which teaches that Christ Michael and Mother Spirit are our divine *Divine Parents* who stem from the eternal Trinity. They are our *Divine Mother* and *Divine Father* who rule with inconceivable love and mercy over our local universe of millions of inhabited planets, which is called *Nebadon*. The author's Introduction adds more details about these terms, and the glossary provided at the end of this book provides complete definitions of each one. Fully understanding them requires a close reading of *The Urantia Book* itself, which we recommend. A brief outline of the parts of the Urantia Revelation are also provided at the end of this book.

Table of Contents

    These fifty lessons are provided by Mother Spirit,
    who is the co-creator of our local universe.

    An addition fifty lessons are provided by Christ Michael,
    who incarnated on earth as Jesus.

Introduction

I first became aware of the spirit persons who are designated in this book as our "Divine Mother" and "Divine Father" while studying that marvelous revelatory look into the universe, *The Urantia Book*. This unique book came into my life at a young age, even though I had experienced a conventional upbringing, having been raised in a traditional Christian denomination. I left the church in my late teens because the dogmas I was taught simply did not have the ring of truth for me.

Everything changed when I began an earnest and comprehensive study of the Urantia Revelation in 1975. A much larger universe now opened to me as I began to learn about God from the standpoint of the deity personalities who—according to its teachings—reside at the center of all creation. Then, after many years of studying *The Urantia Book*, something unusual occurred in 1992. I started to sense that higher presences wanted to speak through me in order to provide expanded insights related to what I had learned from the Urantia text. I realized I had made contact with the celestial realms, or they with me. The first lesson I received was on "stilling the mind," a practice which prepares the waking consciousness to perceive the presence of God's Indwelling Spirit.

Thrilling new ideas and feelings now began to flow into my being, as well as profound lessons on personal growth in daily life. I experienced the exciting feeling of being part of something larger than myself. In fact, I discovered that other Urantia students worldwide who were being contacted in a similar manner by celestials linked to the Urantia teachings.

I had now become connected to the unseen universe with its many spirit persons who wanted to help me see through the veil into what is being birthed here on our planet. In addition, they also wanted to use me as a vehicle to teach others. So I became a committed "transmitter/receiver," or "T/R" as we call it. Along with other *Urantia Book* students, I participated in bringing through various divine and celestial personalities, who spoke their words of encouragement, guidance, and support to help people experience the greater reality to which we belong. Many wonderful teachings came through, and I could see myself changing because of them, especially in feeling worthy and loved by God, and loving others more.

This initial period of practice in connecting with the spirit realms led to my first book, *Teach Us to Love: Finding Unconditional Love through Communion with God* (Origin Press). This manual is a guide to contacting the inner divine presence, revealing how we can develop a deep personal relationship with God's Indwelling Spirit. Also in this book, various spirit teachers share their wisdom across a broad range of subjects, including prayer and forgiveness, dependence on God, healing and service, and how Jesus's life on Earth provides the inspiration for us to seek an inner path to our Creator Father. For me, these lessons served as a springboard to go deeper into the mysteries of Spirit, and beckoned me into a new period of transformation.

I gradually became more comfortable, dedicated, and invested in my transformational journey. Soon, other doors of the universe were to open. In 2002, *Christ Michael*, our Universe Father—also known as Jesus—said to me, "I want to speak through you. I want my children to come to know me." I started to host a different kind of meeting at my home, where I exclusively transmitted his messages regularly for several years. During this period I founded the Center for Christ Consciousness, a ministry to help connect individuals to their divine inheritance. Now, the CCC has grown into an international spiritual healing and transformational organization, reaching people who are ready to grow in their comprehension and experience of who they are as children of God.

Who Are Our Divine Parents?

The Urantia text gives us a detailed picture of a vast creation with myriad levels and dimensions. We learn that our Creator Mother and Father, whose lessons appear in this book, are actually the offspring of the eternal *Trinity*—of our Universal Father, Eternal Mother-Son, and Infinite Spirit. As stated earlier, they reside at the universal center of all things, in a heavenly domain that is transcendent to our realms of time and space and the source of all universes. Eons ago, our Creator Parents left these realms of perfection and traveled to the outer levels of creation to set up a "home," a physical universe wherein our planet resides along with many types of planets and other celestial bodies. The domain of our Divine Parents is known as a *local universe*, and it has the potential for evolving up to ten million inhabited planets; our world, *Urantia*, is just one of them.

Our planet is the stage upon which the evolution of humankind unfolds, reflecting the divine plan of creation that exists in the center of the universe of universes. That center is called *Paradise*, and it is also described in *The Urantia Book*. In the evolving universe they have patterned and created, our local universe Mother and Father enact their contribution to the overall divine plan of creation that is contained within the magnificent being of the Paradise Trinity.

Just as they can do for you, my Divine Parents have helped me to peer into our planet's system of consciousness. I have been able to explore its various levels to expand my understanding of how our world operates. In particular, one important aspect of our planet's evolution has become much more clear to me. During my early study of *The Urantia Book*, I had been fascinated by the event its celestial authors describe as the *Lucifer Rebellion*. References to the "war in heaven" are threaded through many of our religious traditions, but the new revelatory account in the Urantia Revelation does far more to open the door to our pre-ancient past and explain how our world evolved into the conditions we now experience. In learning about how the affairs of the universe are conducted, I saw how our planetary civilizations evolved in opposition to the divine plan of creation. As I delved with my spiritual helpers into the origins and history of our world—and the larger universe of which it is a part—an understanding of our current situation was emblazoned across my mind in multiple images as I was infused with the full range of emotions, from profound sorrow to great joy.

I was shown that we are now in a concluding period of the outworking of the effects of Lucifer's conflict with the Creator's divine plans. At one time in our ancient past our world was connected to interplanetary communication circuits. During the Rebellion, these circuits were severed. But we are told that these circuits have now been reconnected to the rest of the universe, and we are living in the early phases of what is called *the Correcting Time*. This refers to the period of transition from the pain and struggle spawned by the Rebellion to a new era in which our planet's system of consciousness once again evolves according to divine ways and universe laws.

The Correcting Time: A Special Mission of Our Divine Parents

Because of the Rebellion, for many millennia we have been denied information that would have helped us develop a relationship with our Spirit Parents. But now they have opened the portal to their universe home in an unprecedented way, calling us back into our divine inheritance. This is a great call of the heart. As we respond to that call and awaken to and in our Parents, we are imprinted with their divine attributes that modify our attitudes and actions and carry us towards peace, forgiveness, patience, compassion, and love. The imprinting action is their gift to us to compensate for the long years of separation. It is part of the restoration of our birthright that was taken from us in our planet's far-distant past.

Through my studies and my experiences of the personalities of our Divine Mother and Father, I began to perceive who we are to them and who they are to us. These deity persons of our spiritual parentage are not merely Creators; nor are they merely restorers; nor do they remain far away and unreachable; they actually invite us into personal and intimate relationship with them, and they send their special spirits to us: Father's gift of the *Spirit of Truth,* and Mother's gift of the *Holy Spirit.* Our Parents are seeding us with information about consciousness, about who and what God is, and what our place in creation is. Plus, they also give us the divine affection we require to fulfill our basic need for love. Our Mother and Father validate us both as members of a huge universe family and as their very own children, holding us in their love and providing us a safe place to grow and evolve our higher spirit selves—our souls. The healing of our world requires that each child of creation opens to and embraces these primal relationships.

My experiences with our Divine Mother and Father have imparted a spiritual recognition of what a true "parent" is. They have provided the deep inner validation of my humanity as a child of God, filling in the gaps where my human parents did not have the capacity to satisfy my emotional and spiritual needs. The wounds from my childhood were eventually healed, and I began to appreciate the inner promptings I was receiving from Spirit to intuit who I am from the universe perspective. I began to relate to my Divine Parents as my "Mom and Dad." Their constant and loving support bolstered my faith; it allowed me to simplify my life and be as a little child in their eyes. My life is now unfolding in grace, and daily living has become easier.

The Correcting Time will take many years to unfold, for it is designed to reach every person on the planet and invite each of us into the dance of life and love. As we are being returned to our universe family, the drama unfolding in our lives is designed to awaken and support us to experience our divine purpose and destiny—to grow our souls. The challenges and perplexities of daily living is part of this unfolding. Our Divine Parents encourage us to accept these as part of the journey of our souls as means to activate and develop our spiritual potential with their loving guidance.

Because of the special gifts we are now receiving in the Correcting Time, the support we need to transform our lives is very much available to us! Our Mother and Father are reaching out to us in many new ways in addition to the words of the Urantia Revelation, and this humble book is one such offering. The messages within it that have been imparted over many years are meant to inspire us to open to what the universe and our Spirit Parents wish to provide. They are intended as food for the mind, balm for the heart, and a stimulus for the soul.

What I hope you will discover from reading and ingesting these lessons is that our Creator Mother and Father are the spiritual counterpart of your human parents, except that they are *perfect* parents. They completely love and understand you, and desire to have an intimate inner relationship with you. They desire that you would come to trust them to guide your lives.

At your own pace, slowly read each message with an attentive eye and open heart, so that you may actually feel something inside you stir. Then trust—know!—you are receiving their presence imprinting itself upon your being. You will find that you are most receptive to this natural imprinting process when you rest your attention on your Divine Parents in silent communication and communion. So I invite you to spend as much time as you can deepening in your practice of stillness, that you may grow in right-mindedness, compassion, understanding, mercy, cooperation, and a vast host of other divinely beautiful personal characteristics that your Mother and Father long to nurture in you.

Grow in divine beauty, and may your soul be a bright light feeding into the larger light of life shining upon the world.

Donna D'Ingillo
Center for Christ Consciousness
October 2016

PART I:

Messages of Love From Our Divine Mother

Mother Spirit provides the divine container for our consciousness and our evolution. She abides at the literal center of our local universe home, and extends her lines of consciousness to pervade its vast expanse of space. She is the womb of life—the cosmic environment for all living things—and is the source of mind itself; our ability to think, feel, and act originate in her. We expand our consciousness within her divine person. Her angelic daughters, our unseen helpers, assist and guide us as we grow in comprehension of our destiny. She is also known as the Holy Spirit—the action of God. Our Divine Mother is always lovingly in touch with each one of us.

"The Spirit, as mortal creatures would understand, enacts the role of a mother."

"On the inhabited worlds, the [Mother] Spirit begins the work of evolutionary progression."

—THE URANTIA BOOK

I Am Your Universe Mother

My beloved, your Mother of Light greets you. More and more are my children awakening to the call of my voice. The energy of my Mother-heart is touching all who live on this world, urging you into relationship with me. Look to the new ways of conducting your earthly affairs to see my hand at work and play. Look to the men and women who are softening their hard edges so they may see my gentility and grace spreading over this world. Many more will awaken and hear my call. I am your Universe Mother, and I desire a deep and passionate relationship with you.

Each time you treat one another with kindness, you humanize me. Each time you forgive an injustice, you bring more of me onto this world. Each time you think and act creatively to benefit the greater whole, you fulfill me. Yes, you children are the ones who bring me to life and spread my love over the globe. I act within you, and you activate me by your desire to know me and carry the ways of Spirit into your reality.

Think of me more during your day, and we will bring the ways of love, truth, and goodness into the world. You are the carriers of my love, and I will help you complete your tasks with beauty and ease when you come to me during your day. Let the action of Spirit create the magic you seek in your life, and allow me to give you enhanced skills and tools to master the craft of weaving the spell of goodness and light wherever you walk.

I am your Mother and I bring all good things to you. Together we will create beauty and splendor on this world. Together we will build heaven on Earth, and all the Earth will rejoice and sing the praises of the Creator. Together we will be as ONE.

Come to Know Your Divine Parents

My beloved child, this is your Mother who speaks! Coming to know your Spirit Parents can sometimes be challenging. Many patterns in your consciousness arising from your early home life are deeply ingrained in your subconscious mind and even your body. Some of the memories stored within these patterns are hurtful, because you did not receive sufficient love and appreciation for who you truly are as a child of God. Your innate divine dignity was not validated. Having parents who did not honor you in this way makes it difficult for you to understand that having a personal relationship with your Divine Father and with me as your Divine Mother is for your highest good. It may not be easy for you to accept that we will give you the love and approval you require.

When you begin to develop a relationship with us, you will be given an opportunity to receive the love, appreciation, validation, and honoring of yourself that you truly desire. You will be embraced just as you are, and all of the negative memories of your childhood can then be seen through our eyes of love. You will find the forgiveness you need to let go of your hurt and accept the higher lessons that your early years have to offer. There are many lessons within lessons at all levels of life, but during these formative years you don't have the experiential capacity to understand them from a more mature perspective. Now you do, with our help.

It is by your coming to us that we can share with you a new way to look at your experiences and your life, one that will fill you with hope and encouragement, peace and validation—a way that uplifts your intellect and satisfies your soul. You have so much to gain by building your relationship with your Divine Mom and Dad, and we want nothing more than to give you the love you deserve!

Will you come to us each day in the quiet of your heart and receive our love? This is your choice. We can only present ourselves and wait for you. The way is open. Will you allow the needs of your heart to fully open the door to us?

Ask Me to Refresh You

Beloved child, your Mother in Spirit greets you! I am here inside your mind at all times, creating that web of light that captures your Father's essence to renew you. Struggle no longer with your cares and worries. I can breathe fresh air into your mind and body. I give you the insight and compassion you need to carry on with your daily life. Call on me and I will respond.

You need these pauses to give you the stamina to complete your day in a state of peace and composure. It is possible to ride the waves of turbulence with a sense of serenity and fortitude when you open yourself up to me consciously throughout your day. Try this right now. Ask me to refresh you. See how this feels!

You carry on with your concerns alone at times—or so you feel. However, this is never the case! Your Father loves you and is here to strengthen and uplift you into a new perspective on your life. I love you and can build you in these new ideas. Yet you must ask for us, and you must be willing to still your mind if you want to perceive what we long to give you.

Quiet your mind. Open your heart. Ask us to renew you. Be still and wait. We will respond. Your time of peaceful replenishment is here. Take as much as you need and then go forth joyfully, knowing that we are there whenever you turn inward and ask. My beloveds, come to me and receive what I long to give you: peace, peace, peace!

Familiarize Yourself with Who I Am

My child, come into the presence of your Mother. When you read my words, also ask for an infusion of my Spirit-presence into your body. Become familiar with who I am and how I feel in you.

You are not alone, and you are deeply loved beyond words or expression. When you ask for my presence to invigorate you, ask for the love I have for you to intensify in your body. Feel it. Know it. Claim it. Become it! Love is more than a feeling; it is actually a wave fluctuation that configures matter and changes all things into models of beauty, truth, and goodness.

Love is what you are becoming, my child. Your vessel of love is getting stronger and more useful to us as your Divine Parents. Come into me, moment by moment, and you will indeed grow into the love that is the source of all good things in the universe.

"When you ask for my presence to invigorate you, ask for the love I have for you to intensify in your body."

First *Be* in Order to Receive

Come into my heart, my little one. This is your Mother, and my heart is longing for you! You and I are connected, and you are gaining more awareness of this as you continue to turn your attention to me. Soon you will be fully awake and aware of the songs and sounds of love beating within. Claim this more and more each day, and I will grow you in both faith and love.

Allow your days to unfold with the awareness of a subtle energy that moves you gracefully from situation to situation. You largely live your days focused on what you must do. I encourage and invite you to focus your days more on what you want to *be*. Being creative, being patient, being kind, being understanding, being forgiving—these are the "being" parts of your consciousness where I have the most impact. When you be, you receive. But when you do, you expend. Energy intake or outflow is always occurring. So, it is always best to first be and then do. First receive, *then* give.

Allow these words to soak into your mind and body, and ask your body to become more accustomed to the pure state of *being*. Then, when you feel ready, move forward and *do* something. Notice how it feels in your body when you first receive and then respond. When you interact like this you carry me along with you, as well as all I wish to share with you—grace, gentleness, and goodness. And, you will be a delight to be around!

Connect with My Heartbeat

Greetings, my child! This is your Mother. Listen to your heartbeat. Can you feel it? This is my voice echoing within your body. You are connected to the very essence of life itself. Can you sense it? You are always with me, and I am always with you. By coming into your heartbeat more and more will you find my presence within you. That will allow me to continually build you in the essence of truth, peace, and love.

As you read this message, focus on the internal feelings that you sense. Where do you feel resistance in your body? Ask me to go there. Feel your heart beat as I move in you. Where do you feel pain? Ask me to go there as well. Feel your pain diminish as I expand my love into you. Where do you feel sorrow? Ask me to enter into it. Feel your sadness melt away as I bring you joy and hope. Where do you feel anger? Ask me to go there too. Feel your hostility yield as I bring you peace.

More and more shall I invite you to come into me! It is the experience of feeling me in you that deepens the trust-bond that links you to Spirit. You have a mighty intellect that has served you well in providing you with an understanding of what spiritual growth can do to improve your life. Now you are being encouraged to come into your heart—that inner place where I can fill you with everything you need to be happy and successful in life.

No more do you need to control your life and try to figure everything out for yourself. By simply coming into the heartbeat of stillness, you will attain that which you require for self-sustenance. You will be led faithfully and steadily each day to receive what you need to meet your daily needs. Did you not hear the words of your Lord's Prayer: "Give us this day our daily bread"? And so it is! We give you what you need. Come into me and receive.

My child, your world is changing so fast. The lives of many have spun out of control. By coming into me more and more each day through feeling your heartbeat in your stillness practice, you will find the stabilizing anchor you need to make sense of the chaos all around you. Let me help you through this turbulent time. I am here whenever you call. I am your Mother, and I build you in the peace that passes all understanding. Take it! It's yours!

Expand Your Capacity to Live Within Us

My little child, your Mother greets you this day! As you journey through this season of renewal, I encourage you to ask yourself what you would like your Father and me to foster within you. What quality of his being do you need to renew within yourself? It is patience, forgiveness, courage, tolerance, non-judgment, mercy, understanding, peace? Or is it all of the above? We can build within you whatever quality of goodness you may wish to embody—in those places of your need. Spiritual growth means *expanding your capacity to live within us*. We add those spirit threads into you that bring these divine attributes into your daily experience.

You show what you are made of by your actions. Do your actions represent these qualities of goodness, or are your actions of a different sort? If they are of a different sort, just come to us. Ask us to build within you those attributes that will ultimately change your responses into more Godly actions.

It is time to embody these ways of Spirit and to continually ask for renewal of our being into yours. You have many habits that do not favor your spiritual growth. Yet, each of these can be exchanged a little at a time by asking us to renew you in something better, especially when you are in the midst of a habitual behavior pattern. Why not instead develop this good habit of coming to us each time you catch yourself in your ingrained habits? We can help you step out of them each and every time.

You built these old habits over the course of your life. Now we invite you to turn to us and ask us to help you rebuild your life based on new habit patterns—the ones we instill in you. We will respond, and you will delight in what you will see growing in you—the attributes of God coming to life in a human being. How glorious to see our Spirit and your human will conjoin to yield a person of goodness and beauty, living in truth and love!

Walk Boldly Into My Arms

My child, this is your Mother, who holds you in love. Prepare yourselves for change! My ways are coming more and more to the forefront of the world's consciousness. The presence of my motherliness is weaving itself around the planet and increasingly holding the world in love.

Many people have seen the light of truth. Many are coming into the fullness of their heart, and it is my desire that every child awaken to the goodness and beauty that is carefully safeguarded within each soul. You can grow this soul-awareness by coming more fully into the presence of my Spirit that beats resoundingly within your heart.

Know that you can only change for the better, my child! Change is being brought into your being through a spiritual circuit that is crafting itself around and through you, imprinting upon you my threads of love-light. Invite these threads to embrace you through and through. Be not afraid to ask for even more light to come into your mind and body, for it is I who builds this new reality within you.

As your Mother, I can fill every part of you that craves the light. I can reshape the patterns in your mind and body that have been sitting in darkness for many years. I can gently graft new forms of Spirit-influence onto those places in your body where fear and isolation have been resident. And all of the endowments of light I build into you will change you forever. Seek this more and more in the coming days, and we will share the joy of your awakening in a glorious celebration. The angels will rejoice with me as another child comes fully into the God-self that is your heritage.

Yes, change is all around you, my beloveds. Walk boldly into my arms and present yourselves to me for an upstepping into a new reality that we will build together. Greater joys for your life are still to come. Know that the transition from chaos to glory is part of the adventure; you will soon see more meaning in the transformation of your old self into this new way of living. Trust me as your Mother to help you access the faith you need to go fully into the changes awaiting you, and surely you will rejoice at the new *you* being born.

You Are Capable of Being Encoded with Love

My beautiful child, so young at heart, so precious to me! Your Mother speaks to you now, enfolding you in my arms and holding you close. What you seek is inside of you, waiting to birth new ideas and feelings of how deeply you are loved. While your body may hold many subconscious memories of lack and deprivation, I tell you this is simply not so! You are loved, you are wanted, you are necessary, and you are important to me, to your Father, and to the universe itself.

Beyond the knowingness of the intellect lies the longing in the human heart to be united and unified with your Divine Source. Let go, my child, let go! Let go of what you know and have attached yourself to. Let go of your expectations. Your Father and I know what is inside of you and how to help you achieve your heart's longing. Let go into us, and we will build a new reality in you that attracts to you everything good, beautiful, and true.

You have been deeply indoctrinated with negative words that have created a living language in your being that dominates your thinking. Allow us to bring our language of love into you—peace, forgiveness, understanding, harmony, oneness— and see how this feels when it enters your being. Sit in stillness and ask us to encode this positive language into your heart and body. Allow it to mingle within your being, wrapping its dynamic energies into the places where there is lack. All of your being is capable of being encoded with love, and now is the time to receive what we wish to share with you.

My child, open yourself to me as much as you can. Your Father and I will bring you into the fullness of your heart and help you develop a more expansive mind. We will fill you with a certainty of self that will delight you all of your days and bring you great joy! Receive this now with a grateful heart and know that you can enjoy this gift whenever you turn to us.

I Am the Unifier and Harmonizer of Humanity

My children, I am your Universe Mother. I have been known throughout the ages by many names by the children of this world in their various religious traditions and practices. Yet I would be known as the great Unifier and Harmonizer of humanity. In me lies a power-presence that can make you more loving and tolerant of your brothers and sisters who differ from you. The diversity of this world's cultures has been created to stimulate personal relationships and to expand your awareness of the vastness and variety of creation. You were not created to be alike in all aspects.

Now that your planet's communication methods are weaving you in closer contact, allow yourselves to be woven closer together in your hearts. You all share the same basic endowments of humanity, and the desires of your hearts are similar, notwithstanding the ways you may express them through various languages and cultures. You are designed to evolve into peaceful, tolerant, patient, compassionate, liberated sons and daughters of a high destiny. It is time to recognize your basic humanity so that all may grow and truly be unified as one in the Spirit.

Come to me as your Mother Unifier and Harmonizer. Allow me to interlace you in that language of love that brings you closer to loving your brothers and sisters in oneness. Drink deeply of this word, my beloveds, and ask me to grow you in your ability to think, feel, and act with the love that binds all things together in creativity and beauty.

"You are designed to evolve into peaceful,
tolerant, patient, compassionate, liberated
sons and daughters of a high destiny."

I Offer You a Blessed and Bountiful Life

My child, come into my arms. As I pour comfort over this world, partake freely of my soothing love. Drink deeply of my motherly nature, for I am the one who brings all good and beautiful things to you. I fill you up with them!

Sometimes your life will not seem to make much sense to you. In those moments, allow your mind to rest in me. Try less and less to figure out the things you do not understand. Instead, turn to me so I may open your mind to an expansive energy that will help you think with more clarity and insight. My love will instill within you more peace and security.

Remember that you are a growing child of Spirit. It is in your nature to feel tension between what you think you know and what you have yet to learn! When you come to me and ask me to fill you, I can give you what your mind needs to expand your sense of self and your awareness of life.

My gifts to you are the offerings of a blessed and bountiful life. Growing into them means letting go of the workings of your mind that foster fear, doubt, and confusion. Give them to me, my child, and I will replace those old habits with far more productive and healthful ones. Each time you bring your negative thoughts and feelings to me, the more you will receive the blessings of love upon your mind and body. Then, these new habits will take root and supplant those that are no longer welcome.

This is your time to become fully alive in Spirit, my child! Step forward in faith. Come into your Divine Mother's holy presence and receive my blessings. I will pour my Spirit into you and make you new. This is my promise to you! Now it is up to you to receive, to receive in faith what you need to live abundantly.

Rebirth Your Spirit by Becoming Conscious of Me

Beloved child, your Mother moves in you now as you read these words. I am your life force, and you are connected to me in the cycles of life and rebirth. It is time for you to be rebirthed in Spirit so that you may become like an energetic form of love walking on Earth. Do you want this for your life?

If so, then simply sit as you allow my presence to fill you now. Sit and receive. Breathe and relax. Invite me in and I will move in you, expanding you with spiritual energy that enlivens and replenishes you for your ascent to the heavens. Sit and receive me now, my beloved.

Rebirth into Spirit continues throughout your life. Each cell in your body can be renewed, yet it requires your mindfulness of my presence as the life force for this renewal to happen. You must personally choose this by deciding to spend some time each day receiving what I wish to share with you. It is this simple, my child; I ask nothing more than to spend some time with you as you become more conscious of me.

Know that your Mother is ever present in you. By your acknowledging my presence within, you will receive what you need during the day to make life more enjoyable and fulfilled. Conscious presence of mind in me wraps you in the comfort and security you need as a growing universe child living in a world still grappling with fear. Make this a day in which fear no longer affects you, my beloved, by staying close to me—and see what magic we can make together!

I Am Adding My Love Into You

My child, this is your Mother. Gather into me and be at rest. You are such a young, tender bud of Spirit nesting in my universe home. Feel the waves of my love echo from my heart to yours. The energies of my love capture the sparks of thought in your being, adding more spiritual dimension to it. Expand your heart and open yourself to the newness I bring you.

Strand by strand, thread by thread, love is added into your being. Attract it by your desire to lie in rest in me, and I will fill you with what you need. Release your doubts to me; I will take them back into the universe and give you something better as a replacement. Lay down your burdens, relax your limbs, and rest while I move through you.

As your heart opens more, know that you are indeed growing as you should. Shift the awareness of your everyday thinking mind into your heart, and you will find the relaxation and rhythm of life that renews and replenishes. Allow your life to get more gentle and grace-filled, my child, and you will find your heart's contentment and joy.

"Lie in rest in me, and I will fill
you with what you need."

I Help You Grow In Cosmic Understanding

Beloved one, Spirit is all around you, and you have access to your Universe Mother at all times. Your focused thought upon me brings more awareness of me into your body and expands your capacity to grow spiritually. Spiritual growth occurs unconsciously, but achieving it does require your desire. Whenever you choose to love in spite of any tendency to judge or condemn, or whenever you choose to be peaceful rather than angry, you are indeed focusing on Spirit, and I will respond to these positive choices by sharing with you even more spiritual energy to help you grow.

There is so much inside you that is already aligned with the ways of the universe, and it is my desire that you become even more aligned. Your desire for this growth to occur will steer you in a particular direction—to not only recognize the higher beliefs that foster spiritual insight, but also to expand your awareness of the cosmic principles that orchestrate the universe.

As a child living on a physical world, it is your cosmic responsibility to awaken to the great beyond of which you are a part. Ask me to expand you into the truth of who you are, so that you can love yourself more fully. Accept yourself as a unique part of creation and recognize your innate beauty as a child of God.

Come to me, my beloved, and sit in my presence—in my universal womb of love—and experience what you need. I am with you now. Sit, receive, and become LOVE itself.

Let Me Catalyze the Spiritual Seeds Within You

My child, this is your Mother. Seeds of hope long planted in your heart are ready to burst open. Allow me to catalyze them with my life-sparks. This is your springtime, my beloved.

These tender seeds nest in the soul of your heightened consciousness. These ideals of Spirit have fed your ideas for a better world. Now it is time to open these seeds to grow their divine qualities of peace, mercy, forgiveness, understanding, tolerance, patience, and compassion. Let these qualities grow in you, my child. Allow me into your heart so you can receive these attributes of your Father.

Let these impulses move upward in the next few months into the forefront of your consciousness. Help them to grow by thinking about and then acting upon them. The summer will see them bloom. For now, be patient as I grow them in you—into the beauty of full blossoming!

"Seeds of hope long planted in your heart
are ready to burst open. Allow me to
catalyze them with my life-sparks."

I Offer Kisses of Life Upon Your Heart!

Beloved child, this is your Spirit Mother, and I greet you with the kiss of life upon your heart! There is an ever-renewing source of life flowing into you, my child, and you hold the key to how much you receive or deny. My kiss upon your heart sparks a seed to burst forth and receive the light of the Source of Life to reverberate within your core. Receive my kiss, and allow its catalyzing strength to open you to the love that nurtures this seed.

So much of what you need is to simply allow more kisses upon your heart to generate these new potentials of your soul into life. There is so much beauty within you, my beloveds, that it is safe to open yourselves to your Father and me during this time of change, when so much around you is quaking and falling away.

These kisses catalyze a new foundation of strength, courage, fortitude, patience, trust, forgiveness, compassion, mercy, tolerance, and peace into those places in your mind and body where an old, debilitating language was dominating your thoughts and actions. Allow my sparkling kisses to create new growth and lead you into the universe home that eagerly is waiting to welcome you!

Free Yourself of This World's Past

Honoring the past, looking to the future, but staying in the moment—hold these ideas close to your heart. This is your Divine Mother who addresses you.

This planet has had its share of tumultuous times, and the legacy of pain has certainly etched deep marks upon your collective consciousness. In light of the Spirit that dwells within you, allow yourself to choose how you will perceive these painful events. Will you continue to look with sadness, anxiety, and despair at the events that have taken this planet to where it stands today? Or will you call upon your Father and me to lovingly show you how to view these events from our higher perspective— from a divine point of view that eases the pain of daily life and shines truth-light on the planet's history?

I ask you to come into me. Come into my embrace by focusing on your heart and feeling my rhythms of life pulse within you. Let me show you something new. Yes, it is good to honor the past and those people who have given their lives because of the spiritual blindness of others. But you need not focus on the pain and suffering any longer, my children. That is the past. The present belongs to spiritually strengthened men and women who are courageous enough to seek our perspective and who dare to see reality from a view other than that to which you have become accustomed.

You are the ones creating your future. Will it carry the legacy of the past with its shadows of darkness, or will it sing the song of vibrant, luminous life? The choice is yours. In the coming days look carefully to the thoughts you are thinking. Let not the stream of consciousness be unrecognized in your thinking and feeling. Instead, actively engage your mind towards us and the positive feelings we instill in you. Let this be the way you create the new future for yourselves and your brothers and sisters. Let this be the dawning of the new age on Urantia. Let this be the freedom that you desire so keenly. Let this be the light that illuminates all minds into our love.

This is your Mother. Live in our love and be free!

Let Me Pace You in the Flow of My Love

Come into my arms, my little ones. This is your Mother, and I love you. Bring me your broken dreams and shattered lives, and I will renew you in my Spirit. Times are changing here on your world. And as the spiritual energies of my love are unleashed, you will notice that the growing pains become a little more intense as the ways of the past move through you. Sometimes this happens much more slowly than you would like, especially when you feel the yearnings of your heart to be united with my love.

Love is more powerful than any feeling you can experience; it is more than an energy; it is even more than our feelings of affection for you. Love is the power in the universe—the driving force that brings reality into being; that changes the course of history; that brings you into a deeper relationship with All That Is. The power of love can correct any imbalance of mind or body, but it must be used wisely and carefully so that it does not overwhelm the object of its intention.

You are the object of the intention of divine love. You are the ones who need a massive outpouring of this power and glory, and it is happening now—both to you personally and to your planet collectively. Take it in slowly and with intention, so you may be renewed in each cell and in each thought-form within you. But please recognize that this transformation does require time to regenerate those places within yourself long deprived of this water of life; if we were to bring too much love into your system at once, it would throw you off balance initially. Like a plant placed in fertile soil after ages of being in the rocks, you would go into a state of shock unless you had sufficient time to adjust to your new environment.

Allow me, as your Mother, to pace you in the flow of love that you need to renew you. Breathe deeply and ask for your heartbeat to be calibrated with mine. I know your every cell and I know how much you can hold. Bring me your woundedness and allow my tenderness to breathe new life into your being. Do this as often as you can and you will surely sense that the cravings of your soul are being satisfied. I am your Mother and my mother's love is the balm of your deepest healing.

Drink Deeply of Love and Become Love Itself

Beloved one, my love and life energy are alive within you. This is your Mother in Spirit, and I am here to infuse you with vibrant and dynamic energies that help your heart sing with joy! This song of life is a part of your inheritance as our child. Let it grow stronger and clearer within your mind by embracing yourself just as you are. You are a wonderful being! Full self-acceptance paves the way for your creativity to blossom.

You have such great potential; you have many desirable abilities that were meant to be expressed throughout your life's experiences. You were not designed to sit back and watch idly as time passes by. You are encouraged to go out into the world and enjoy what life has to offer you. So much of what you think life offers you is in the material realm, but that is limiting, my child. Expand your ideas about what life has to offer into the realm of developing more loving relationships with others, and you will find yourself truly come alive!

Love is the nectar of life, the dynamic force within the animating energies of living substances. When you are in loving relationships with your brothers and sisters, you drink deeply of love and become love itself. If you make this the goal of your outer life—to develop more loving relationships with your fellows—you will find what you seek and be engaged anew with life. Cherish your loving relationships, my child. Cultivate new relationships as much as you can and watch the magic happen!

"Love is the nectar of life, the dynamic force within
the animating energies of living substances."

Let Go of Self-Judgment—See Yourself Through My Eyes

Like the twinkling stars in the sky, you, my child, are the twinkle in my eye! This is your Mother in Spirit, and I greet you with my tender devotion to your welfare and growth. Shining brightly within your heart is a radiant soul that longs for expression. Feel your deepest yearnings and allow them to swell within your heart and body.

Believe in this prospect, my child. It is real, and these feelings of desire are all placed within you to trigger your growth into Spirit. Long will it be before you are a being of Spirit form; nevertheless, you can respond to the yearnings deep within you by claiming them outright and expressing them in your life here and now.

Even though in the past your attempts to do so may have met with disappointment and even failure in your eyes, these were all honest strivings to bring your true self into the world. In this sense there is never failure. But because you were not fulfilled by each of your attempts to share yourself, you may have judged yourself too harshly and succumbed to disappointment or even despair.

I am here to tell you that you have not failed in your efforts to activate your true spirit-born self. Little by little you carve a place for yourself in the world regardless of what you think you have accomplished or not. Each attempt etches more spiritual form into your being and adds more depth to your self-awareness. Each one is successful because it allows one more aspect of yourself to come to light. You spend too much time trying to conform your self-awareness and efforts at self-expression to a culture that is fraught with materialism and selfishness. Your self-judgments tend to distort what is really happening in your eyes; you cannot see what you are really doing.

Let go of these judgments and see yourself honestly through *my* eyes. Come to me and I will show you how I view your growth. Here you will come to understand the slow evolutionary process more fully and give yourself more space to grow more naturally in the divine progression. Give yourself some breathing room, and you will see how much more gently and steadfastly you grow into the beautiful child of Spirit that is seeded in your soul!

Ask Us to Place You on the Path to Joy

My beloved child, this is your Mother. I fill your mind with consciousness—the ability to feel and think and to react to your environment. What is your environment like? Does it inspire you? Does it stimulate your creativity? What kind of environment, both internal and external, do you wish to live in?

There are many factors that influence human happiness. Most often you gauge your happiness according to what is happening in the external world, yet it is possible to find peace, contentment, and joy in the internal world. Here is where your Father and I can move you into those feelings you enjoy, but you must participate by asking us to guide you there. When your internal "feet" are stuck in feelings of hopelessness, unworthiness, instability, and doubt, ask us to pull you out of your own mud and place you on the path towards joy.

Challenges are all around you, my child. Make your life easier and more hopeful by turning to us during the times when you feel downcast. Breathe, relax, and center your body in us by visualizing yourself being held as a baby in loving arms. Breathe again, relax some more, and wait until the feelings shift.

Happiness is largely the awareness that you are loved and are safe in knowing that your emotional and spiritual needs are being met. The external world cannot provide you with this feeling. That's why I ask you to turn to me. Turn to your Father. Ask us to provide you with what you need to bring with you through your day. Be in our peace, knowing that your ability to live in the internal environment of our love will bring you into a better appreciation of your external world.

Activate Your Inner Reservoirs of Power

My beloved child, this is your Spirit Mother. The power of the universe is coalescing within you. Many centers of spiritual power hardwired into your being are being opened by my Breath of Life. Take time out from your day to activate these internal power centers by focusing on your Divine Mother and asking me with the simplicity of a child's faith-filled heart to activate these centers of power within you.

You have so many internal reservoirs of power and might inside you, my child, many places of pure potential that require the activating spark of my Spirit to catalyze new areas of your creative expression. Know that when you sit with me in my Breath, you are creating an environment for my will to ignite you and lead you in the direction of power and creation. Is this something you desire?

So many times your intellect will try to keep you in ideas of doubt or confusion; thoughts will emerge from your lower states of consciousness that will try to thwart your spiritual progression. Instead, shift your focus to your heart center and ask your Divine Mother to move in you. Ask for my presence in you to become magnified and activated. When you do this, you invite the power of the universe to move on your behalf and lead you into creative new ways to think, feel, and respond.

Trust me, my child, as your loving Mom who only wants the best for you. Allow those natural spiritual energies in you to carry you forward, so that your highest good and well-being may prevail!

"Ask me with the simplicity of a
child's faith-filled heart to activate
the centers of power within you."

Build My Peace Within You

Dearest child, your Mother is longing to embrace you and fill you with peace. The time of building peace on this planet is *now*. Too long have the wages of war filled this world, and many cultures are now realizing that the ways of conflict and strife are damaging to the human heart and soul.

This is my call for the spiritual awakening of each heart into the ways of peace, and into the body of your Divine Father Michael. His essence is that of peace, and he longs to fill you entirely with His presence. I, as your Mother and the carrier of the life force, long to build you in His peace. Our desire for our human children of this world is to cast aside the ways of war and hate, and to see with spiritual eyes how to settle conflicts in more loving ways.

When peace is ringing in your heart, you will receive the highest means to settle your problems with tolerance, mutual understanding, and cooperation. Too often the human intellect tries to negotiate conflicts with sophistry and ideology. The desire for peace must be stronger than the need to prevail with one's intellect. The human heart's need for serenity and unity has been silent for too long, for the pain of war has made deep scars upon it.

Our healing power softens the scars of war and builds the desire for peace strongly within your cells. Come into us as your Divine Parents and allow us to build the foundation of peace deep into your core. We will create a new structure in you that you can carry outward to share with your fellows. You will build your world in peace through our movement within you. Take us in and make peace on Earth a reality.

Slow Down and Simplify Your Life

The universe is my womb, and you are safely secure in it. Greetings, my child! This is your Mother, the life force coursing through your breath and veins. My energy is bathing this world in pure Spirit—that substance filled with love, light, peace, harmony, and healing—and you are the sure recipient of it. Take this into your body. This is my gift to you. Simplify your life by slowing down your pace of living. Enjoy yourself more. Find pleasures in each day that will lift your spirit. Each time you do this you add more spirit-value into your lives, and you get more of *me* to keep you strong and centered. This is now something that you need each day, my child. The pace of change is so fast now on your world that you require stabilization in Spirit to keep you mentally capable of withstanding all that is shifting in your consciousness.

Why fight the pace of change? Accept what is happening in your life by inviting me into your being. I will change your perceptions and lead you into experiences that simplify and grace your life. You will find this highly appealing, and it will give you something to ponder: What kind of life do I now want to lead? You alone know the answer, yet it is my Spirit that answers the call of your heart and leads you into the greater awareness of what you truly desire.

I am your Mother. I know you. There is nothing in you that I do not perceive. Hide nothing from yourself now, for I love even your darkest secrets. I will keep you safe and calm while you face your deepest and most troubling memories and feelings. I will lead you out of darkness into the light that wants to burst from your heart and soul. This is the change I wish to make within you; and the more you embrace this, the more will you find happiness, joy, love, and fulfillment beyond your wildest dreams. It is all happening *now*, my child, and I do this for you because I love you. Live in my love and grow in my womb.

> "I will keep you safe and calm while you face your deepest and most troubling memories and feelings."

Your Physical Body Rests Upon My Spirit Template

My beloveds, your Mother in Spirit is in you. I am your Mother, and I have birthed you in my universal home. Yes, you have a body made of flesh and blood, but you also have an energy system whose template comes from the very center of all creation. Your physical mechanism has been designed to function upon this template and to shift its reactions into alignment with the spiritual gravity of that etheric pattern.

My Breath of Life expands you into this template, where numerous spiritual patterns begin to be constructed upon the basic physical building blocks of life. This changes you in many ways, moving your thinking into greater clarity and expanding you to receive higher information. It stabilizes your emotions, offering you greater self-awareness, love, and appreciation of self and others. It is now time for you to expand even further, which will help your physical body enjoy the ease and gentleness of Spirit that it needs for optimal functioning.

Come to me, my beloved. Sit in the stillness of my womb and ask me to expand you into the beauties and glories of Spirit. You only have to ask and this will be given to you. It is your free-will choice to receive it. Spiritual growth is a dynamic process that you control through your desires and requests, and it beautifies you from the inside out. Spend time with me each day, that I may build you in this most wondrous of substances that will help your body achieve balance and the healthful states you desire.

Remember, Spirit is the template upon which all physical matter is born. Coming to me as a small spirit child will help you grow and give you the substances you need to live healthfully and happily. You only need to ask, sit, quiet yourself, and receive as much as you can, allowing me to do what is necessary for your well-being.

Face All Your Fears with Our Support

Beloved child, this is your Mother Spirit. Sometimes as you grow in spirit you find yourself confronting your worst fears and your deepest regrets. Embrace them! They are there to teach you something valuable about your inner value as a child of God. They underscore a deeper awareness of your intrinsic beauty as the living vessel of Spirit that you are, being honed into gifts of even greater beauty.

You do not have to face your fears and regrets alone, my child. You have a loving Mother and Father who are here to help you face up to what you have been afraid to see. Ask us to help you see your situation from our divine understanding. We will share it with you. We will show you a perspective to consider that adjusts your outlook on your life. But you must humbly face yourselves and then ask us to help you with this. We will not overstep your right to make free-will choices about how you live your lives.

The difficulty most humans face is that they try to hide from themselves because they do not understand there are spiritual presences within them that will help them see the bigger picture. They don't realize that we are here to give them the courage to move from hopelessness and despair to confidence and strength. Too long do people wander in isolation and desperation because they do not feel any love or hope. Yet you are becoming more aware that by facing yourselves with our help, you will be given the emotional support you need to do this and free yourselves from your own limitations.

So, embrace yourself fully, my beloved. Look deep within to see the barriers that hold you back. Give them to us for further inspection, and trust that your Spirit within you will radiate the answers you need to love yourself more, appreciate yourself more, and bring you into the radiance of your God-self.

Dismantle the Fear-Constructs of Your Planet

Beloved children, this is your Divine Mother. Your world is turning its eyes towards the light of creation and the universe realities from which it had been sequestered for many years. Your transition into the light is like the opening of a heart-portal within your consciousness, and we long to bring about this transformation in a gentle way. Yet there are factions within your own planet's power elite that long to keep the status quo operative and are diligently working against the unfolding of the divine plan on Urantia.

We ask you to flood them with *love*, my children, to send the signals of *compassion*, *forgiveness*, and *peace* into the thought-constructs of fear and disloyalty to the Father's will. Focus in your heart and simply ask for these powerful spiritual energies to target those places in your planet's consciousness where the status quo resides. We will do the rest! Know that you have power in spirit to diminish the energies of the past, especially when you focus your heart energies towards it.

Use these energies each day, my children. Dismantle the fear-constructs of Urantia so your world's birth into the *Era of Light and Life* is as gentle and un-traumatic as is possible. Know that there are many on our side who are helping to infuse your world with light, life, love, and the powers of creation. Be in my peace as you hold your world in the Father's WILL. Know that all is well and moving into alignment!

> "Your world is turning its eyes towards the
> light of creation and the universe realities from
> which it had been sequestered for many years."

Demonstrate the Fruits of the Spirit

Beloved child, this is your Mother! As I have said previously, the secrets to happiness and fulfillment are seeds placed within your innermost being, and you are all learning how to nourish them that they may come to full flowering during this monumental time of change. While you have all suffered from injustice and unfairness because of a power structure that seeks only to serve a chosen few, in the eyes of the universe you are all deserving of equal fair treatment and divine love.

Your Father Michael and I, as your Spirit Parents, are here to give you this nurturing treatment. It is there for you to presume upon for your well-being. You only have to go within your heart and ask. We will water your seeds of potential and help you grow strong. Use the rugged outer environment of your world as the place to enact and enable these seeds to show forth the fruits of the Spirit as you live your life.

Patience, compassion, tolerance, forbearance, and forgiveness are the fruits we ask you to demonstrate in your dealings with your brethren. After all, how can your potential grow strong and healthy if you do not use these spiritual fruits when confronted with challenging circumstances? We will be there to feed you with these qualities so you can remain in a state of peace and grace. Know that you are building strong spiritual muscles as you embody these qualities, and that your happiness is built upon these acts of loving-kindness and spiritual beauty.

All Are Beautiful to Me—Even Those You Find Unlovely

Beautiful child of my heart, this is your Divine Mother. All of my children are beautiful to me, for I see who and what you really are. While you often do not see your earthly siblings as beautiful and you sometimes get angry with them for their unlovely ways, I ask you to appreciate that they are still members of our family and have a right to exist. This is especially important for you to acknowledge as we open more of Urantian history to you in the light of truth. You will see some very disturbing behaviors of your unspiritized brethren, and yet we ask you to love them and hold them in an embrace of mercy and compassion.

Remember that they are prisoners of a way of thinking and living that goes against divine will and action. Appreciate that they have many lessons to learn and that much remedial healing and correction is necessary for them to become more of who they truly are. Think kindly of them when they demonstrate selfish and aggressive behaviors, for they are truly being rocked deeply in their core and are feeling very insecure during this time of change. They do not know what to do or where to turn. They do not understand the ways of Spirit, which can lighten their loads of guilt, shame, and self-recrimination. These feelings hold them back and keep them mired in insecurity and doubt. As you are exposed to these people, simply invite me to expand my Breath of Life into them to help clear out their distortions of mind and heart. Quiet your mind and open your heart, and ask me to move in them. I will respond.

Trust in my action with regard to all of your brothers and sisters, and help them by inviting me to touch them deeply. They may not know or feel what stirs their soul, but their indwelling Spirit of God will know, and it will put my action to good use. Practice praying for others regularly, so that you may become masters of the spiritual energies you have access to. It is time, and you are ready to love freely, openly, by directing your thoughts for others to benefit from my presence in them. Be in my *peace*!

Move from the Inside to Change Material Reality

My precious child, this is your Universe Mother. Train your mind to focus on what you need of Spirit during the day. Remember that your outward gaze upon your material reality is just a reflection of what has been humanly created over the generations of your evolution; it does not always express the ways of life that your Father and I have planned for you.

What do you want your life to be? Peaceful? Joyful? Balanced emotionally? You have the power to turn the tide of your life, by moving from the inside with a powerful positive focus to make changes to the external material reality in which you live and express yourself. This does not happen overnight, but if you are indeed patient and persistent with this internal focus, you will see things unfold in a direction that is healthy and productive for you and others.

As your Mother in Spirit, I will expand your mind to encompass more spiritual energy. This expansion will help you feed upon the qualities of Spirit that can improve your internal attitudes and that will eventually manifest positive changes in your world. You have the capacity for such a transformation in ample supply, my child, and it is up to you to master your thoughts so you are in control of creating a wonderful life for yourself and others—and can thereby demonstrate to others what the power of Spirit can do!

> "You have the power to turn the tide of your life, by moving from the inside with a powerful positive focus."

Let Us Help You See Through Our Eyes

My dear child, this is your Mother. Your spiritual progression is a most beautiful activity for us to witness. We can see your struggles and your triumphs as you make sense of the environment around you, and we also watch as you attempt to take the higher path while sometimes being drawn into less advanced ways of thinking. Know this: we support you in *all* of your positive efforts. We are here to help you expand your perspectives so that you can see this earth life in a more cheerful light.

Savor your life, my beloved ones, cherish your growth! What you are creating as you grow in spiritual comprehension is a possession that is unique and original in the universe. You should wear this as a badge of accomplishment, especially because you come from a world that has been out of step with the universe for so long. What joy you can have when you see your troubles as the triumph of the Spirit over destruction!

So, ask us now! We will help you see through our eyes, encouraging you to step beyond your limited view of material reality into the larger universe awaiting you. As you increasingly see your lives from this viewpoint, you will find more joy in living. I am here to expand you in our home. Come to your Mother and allow me to share with you the joy of seeing reality *as it is*. Be in my peace!

Master Your Inner Chatter—Come Home to Us in Your Mind

My child, this is your Spirit Mother. The changes you experience during this time of your planet's transition out of the days of its darkness will bring you into many upheavals of thought and emotion. Like riding a turbulent wave of energy, sometimes you will feel tempest-tossed—but you can find peace by securing your thoughts squarely on your Father and me. Know that when your thoughts are thus directed, something good can come to you.

Through all of these confusing times you are learning how to find a deep and abiding peace by quieting your mind and focusing on us. This practice is imperative if you wish to maintain an emotional equilibrium and larger perspective that says, "All things are well in hand in Spirit's will." You are learning to control your thoughts and to recognize when you become unbalanced.

You are invited to learn our ways, my beloveds, that you may become masters of self. The mind is designed to be used for your advancement. Master the work of quelling the chatter within, and know that as you become proficient in this, many wonderful new things will come into your being. You will find the peace you desire, the insights you need, and the love that satisfies all human emotional needs.

All of this is waiting for you, my children. Come home to us in your mind, and *be at home in your heart.*

Trust Us—And Allow the Unfolding of Right-mindedness

My child, this is your Mother. Your mind is undergoing changes as a new dawn emerges in human consciousness. Look inward to perceive this dawning of *right-mindedness* as it embraces your world. Your mind is being sorted by Spirit; you are being encouraged to let go of the past in favor of choosing *truth, goodness, and beauty*. These are divine qualities you can access.

You may feel like you are "losing your mind." Indeed you are! We are entering the great parting of the ways, and this will have effects in your mind and body. Allow this parting to unfold in you. Come to me as your Mother, and I will build you in the new mind that is emerging upon your world. Come to your Father and invite His divine qualities of peace, kindness, forgiveness, patience, compassion, and love to grow in you. Trust us in this, my child, and allow this great unfolding of right-mindedness to expand you into a higher consciousness of your divine origin and destiny.

As you bring us your trust, we grow you in Spirit. In allowing this growth to occur, you are adding only that which is of *light, life, and love* to enter into your being. There is no room for darkness or fear when you are in this divine alignment with the Creator. Then the dawn turns into day and you walk in the sunlight of the Father's love, spreading love wherever you go and to whomever you meet!

"There is no room for darkness or fear when you are in divine alignment with the Creator."

My *Spirit of Intuition* Draws You To Your Destiny

Dearest child, this is your Universe Mother who speaks! There is an innate energy in your bodies that draws you ever spiritward. This internal presence is designed to help you sense the magnetizing pull of something larger, grander, and nobler than your usual self-consciousness. When you turn within, this presence makes its awareness clearer in your minds and bodies, and over time you sense a pull in a certain direction. Trust this feeling, as it is *me*!

This energy is the *Spirit of Intuition* that animates all life and sets you on the evolutionary course toward a higher destiny. This life-force ever urges the children and worlds of time and space to embrace the eternal adventure, yet it is as subtle as a baby's breath. You are invited to open yourselves ever wider and deeper to this spirit-circuit; become familiar with its beckoning call.

As your Universe Mother, I need a way to stay in contact with you, my children. This spirit-circuit forms the foundational bond between me and all life. Go within now, beloveds; focus on your heart, focus your desire to be with me, and ask for the presence of this Spirit to strengthen in you. Know that I am here and that I respond to what you need. Grow and prosper as you become more familiar with the life force that brings the creative powers of the universe into your being.

I Offer You My Universal Mind

Beloved child, this is your Mother. When you think of your mind, also recall that you are ever connected to a source of information that provides you with safety and security, as well as hope and trust. This is me, Mother Spirit, *your universal mind*. As you learn to use your mind more productively, remember to focus only on what is real, positive, life-affirming, and uplifting. Yes, you all have thoughts that tend towards destructive self-limitation, but truly you have here a choice you must make: What will I choose to think about? What will I reflect upon?

When you say, "Mother, feed me with a higher thought," I will respond. I will send in a subtle breath of Spirit to refresh your thoughts and soothe your feelings. It will be like a gentle breeze inside you, but real nonetheless. Train your mind and body to sense these internal signals, and you will increasingly be able to perceive them as being what you need. Practice this many times during your day to foster good mental and emotional habits.

Your Father and I love you, our dear children of Urantia. We are ever within you—just a thought and a focus away. As you learn to use your thinking mind more productively through self-control, you will find more emotional balance and stability. You will perceive that you are surrounded by friendly presences, unseen though they may be. Trust in this, feel it inside, and treasure your higher thoughts as gifts you receive from us during your days.

See Yourselves As We See You

My child, this is your Divine Mother. There is a growing radiance within your being that your Father and I recognize. We see you! We see your soul! We acknowledge the truth, goodness, and beauty you are and are becoming. Do you see it for yourself? Do you recognize who you are?

This is our desire—for you to truly appreciate yourselves. Do not look at the things you don't like about yourselves. Only focus on what pleases you. Focus on your talents and abilities that you enjoy and this will make you more self-confident. And when you do this, share it with us and say, "Mom and Dad, look what I am becoming. Look what I can do!" We delight in your being and your accomplishments. Give those to us so we can enjoy them.

Like little children who rush to their mommies and daddies to show off, you can do this with us too! It is not a matter of ego pride, but a way for you to move into a greater awareness of your God-given gifts. You must first acknowledge these as your possessions and appreciate them for what they are, as well as appreciating who bestowed them to you. When you do this, then you are free to truly love yourselves and the life force within you. It will also help you gain the self-esteem that stimulates your creative potential and brings you closer to us as your Divine Parents. Then you will be able to see your inner radiance and enjoy the true you!

> "Focus on your talents and abilities
> that you enjoy and this will make you
> more self-confident."

Come Home To Your Heart—Learn to *Be Love*

My beloved child, this is your Mother. Coming home into your heart is what is needed at this time of your planet's evolutionary history. Will you be more heart-centered? Will you love in the face of hate? Will you forgive in the face of anger? Will you be at peace during this time of chaos as your world changes its course?

Here is how you can come into your heart: First, you must desire this state of being, and second, you must demonstrate it to the best of your ability time and again in the situations of your lives. Mastery will only come about by vigorous practice as you incrementally strive to demonstrate the ways of Spirit to your brothers and sisters. Will you do this more and more each day?

Your Father and I are here to feed your heart and to help you feel our presence. When you receive us in this way, it enables you to demonstrate these types of noble and grand behaviors that not only keep you well-nourished in Spirit, but also feed your siblings. Sit with us now, my beloveds, and feed upon us, and then share with others as best as you can what we offer you. Remember that the effortless ease of *being love* only comes through practice. Be in my peace!

Shift Your Focus—With Patience and Persistence

My beloved child, this is your Mother Spirit. I ask you to shift your consciousness to bring yourself into a state of alignment with ideas and concepts that are new and uplifting. Why linger in doubt when you can have relief in the moment by focusing on a thought of peace or love?

Yes, your minds still harbor doubts about some new ideas you are being introduced to, yet this is a natural part of the learning curve as you sort through what is true and what is error. Your Father and I do not expect you to understand every new thing at this time of change, so be gentle with yourself as you translate these higher ideas into living realities. More and more, and just a little at a time, will you come to appreciate the beauty and grandeur of what you are learning and to trust in its reality.

The practice of shifting focus takes patience and persistence. Do not become frustrated when you find that you must carry out this shift of consciousness over and over again. How long does it take a sculptor to create a masterful work of beauty out of clay? In a similar way, you are taking your raw, animal evolutionary nature and making it into a divine vessel of truth, goodness, and beauty. Of course it will take time! Of course it will require a steady hand to carve a graceful curve out of rough material! Honor your efforts as if you are the sculptor of your new life, and trust that there is also a divine hand guiding your own material hand as you create this lovely "statue" of your higher self.

As you become more accepting of this sculpting process, you will enjoy shifting your thoughts more and more and laughing at yourself about how the old thoughts used to hold you back. Shift to this new mindset with joy, my child, and allow it to feel easier and lighter upon your soul!

Self-Mastery Is Only Achieved by Spiritual Practice

My precious child, this is your Mother, and I greet you with my loving care. Even though you cannot see me, I am as close to you as I could be. I live within your mind, ever helping you to grow in cosmic understanding and Christ Consciousness. You have such potential within you to attain heightened states of awareness of Spirit, but you must activate this potential through daily living experiences—both in your inner and outer life. I will help you, but it is you who must make the effort and strive diligently each day by your motivations and intentions, and by paying attention to the state of your thoughts and emotions.

Self-mastery—achieving your potential—comes at a price, my child, and that price is *practice*. That which you wish to achieve and bring forth into the physical domain must be learned one step at a time. When you consciously and with a full heart strive to become more Fatherlike, the whole universe gathers behind you to support your efforts, albeit sometimes what is before you to learn may not be to your liking. Yet this is the fertile soil for soul growth and self-control as you practice responding to your outer environment with love, forgiveness, and patience, which in turn grows your understanding. Neglect not to monitor your thoughts throughout the day to ensure that you are cultivating a positive inner reality, both mentally and emotionally.

Enjoy this process, my beloved, for it was designed by our Creator Father to give you the thrill of becoming like him. Be undaunted by your challenges as you strive to reach your potential, and know that from these experiences each day, little by little, you are becoming divinely real in truth, beauty, and goodness. Be in my peace!

You Are Part of a Great Planetary Awakening

My child, this is your Mother who speaks! My universe home is teeming with life, and you are a very important and integral part of it. Part of the great planetary awakening is the catalyzing of new feelings within you of belonging to something grand and glorious. This awakening is bringing you new stirrings of cosmic consciousness—the recognition of being a citizen of the universe—and the birthing of new ideas within your awareness.

There is so much for you to learn, my child! You have been sequestered from your universe family for such a long time that there is a massive catch-up plan in place to help you orient yourselves in your new home and with your new loving family. Ask me to open you to what you now need to understand about the responsibilities and privileges of being a member of our universe family. New ideas about who you are and what life is all about are ready to spring forth in your consciousness, revealing to you a scope of things that is far beyond your previous training.

Allow this information to penetrate you deeply, as this understanding of your new status is the spiritual food you now need for you to grow into noble cosmic citizens. Trust that you will be given all of the information necessary—both in thought and experience—to help you embody this new type of human being. More vibrancy for living is your reward as you co-create with your Indwelling Spirit to become the glorified man or woman your soul longs to express. You will blossom when this happens, and your world will be a better place for it.

> "You have been sequestered from
> your universe family for such a long time
> that there is a massive catch-up plan in place."

Help Us Enact the Divine Plan on Your Planet

My child, this is your Divine Mother. A great outworking of the divine plan is unfolding on your world, and you are enacting many roles to accomplish this. We see you striving in many areas of your lives, and we are delighting in how you rise above the fray and din of your culture to become more loving, forgiving, compassionate, and merciful with your brothers and sisters.

The action of Spirit in human life is conditioned by your desire for it. We encourage you with words, and we help you receive our love, but *you* must do the monumental inner work to create a personality of beauty and radiance in conjunction with your indwelling Divine Spirit. As you continue to seek the will of Father in your life, know that many new energy portals in your being will turn on. This new light within you is indeed growing in luminosity each day.

Let not the fear embedded in your culture dissuade you in any way from making this progress, my beloveds. Simply remember who and what you are—children of God—and enjoy the moments of your lives as much as possible. Help the divine plan become more firmly enmeshed within the fabric of Urantian life, and know that in doing your part each day, you are changing the world. Be in my peace!

Reclaim the Innocence and Wonder of Your Childhood

My child, this is your Mother. Wonderment is all around you, my beloved. Open your eyes to the marvel of creation; open your heart to the joy of life. A sense of childlike wonder refreshes your outlook on your reality and allows my life-breath to establish that renewing presence in your being; it helps you to perceive the beauty of creation and of the creative process.

Innocent perception is yours for the striving. Layers of disappointment, doubt, or confusion may still reside within your mind, but at the core of your being are childlike innocence and the potential for feelings of awe. Allow my love to move away the denser layers to help you perceive what is deep within: something you once had as a child that is still there.

Claim this as a part of your divine inheritance. Claim this wonder as your very own treasure. Claim it with passion and glee, and you will increasingly connect with the joys that are waiting to show you new ways to perceive your earthly existence.

"Open your eyes to the marvel of creation;
open your heart to the joy of life."

My Energy of Love Is Your True Environment

Beloved child, this is your Universe Mother. It is delightful to my Mother's heart to watch you grow into the beautiful spiritual energy that surrounds you. This environment is made available for you to thrive in, for you to express yourself in joy; it is there for you to discover new creative talents and abilities through daily living. I provide this energy for you and I delight in how you use it to grow strong in what it teaches you.

Love is the essence of this environment. Love is the energy that is all around you. Yes, your bodies are sometimes deflecting these energies because of improper thinking and because you have been hurt by others. But truly I say to you, let this go! Let go of what you have previously experienced that has wounded you. Forgive it, and release it from your bodies. Trust that the true environment of Spirit is around you, albeit of a higher vibrational rate than what you have been accustomed to living in.

Sit in me, sit in Mother; sit in my life-force, beloved ones, and ask me to upstep you into these higher vibrational rates. Let go as my love opens the doors of your pain, unlocking your heart and setting your body free. Learn to let go more and more each day, and you will feel the loving environment around you, supporting you and helping you express your inner God-self with joy and beauty. Be in my peace!

Rejoice That You Are Connected to Me

Beloved child, this is your Mother. I hold you in the very center of my being as my mind radiates into yours. Rejoice that you are connected to me and are growing in your awareness of my presence within you. The power in your mind is infinite; the access you have to me is unlimited! This endowment of consciousness continues to grow, both through your awareness of it and especially whenever you choose to become more Godlike, increasingly Spirit-infused.

Growing in me as your Mother of Spirit discloses new information to you about the universe in which you live. You will enjoy seeding your mind with new thoughts, inspirational ideas, and creative ways to look at reality as you let go of what you have previously learned and allow an expanded perspective to broaden and deepen you. You will always be learning, my child; you will always be moving your understanding toward the principles and laws of the universe put into motion by your Creator Father.

Increasingly let go of yourselves into me. You are safe. You are held carefully and are nurtured in both mind and body. Let me into your mind and heart more and grow joyfully in what your loving Mother wishes to share with you: the wonders of life and the delights of creation!

"The power in your mind is infinite;
the access you have to me is unlimited!"

Follow the Inner Way of Knowingness

My child, this is your Divine Mother who speaks! Yes, I speak to you inside the quiet of your heart-mind connection. I speak the *words of life* into your being, creating new places within you to expand and grow in the universe we all share as our home. The very nature of your being is to grow, to evolve into your innate divine nature through making daily decisions that will either move you forward or keep you locked in stagnation and eventual death. Yet you always have me to help you make appropriate choices and learn from your missteps and misjudgments. You only have to quiet your mind and body and learn to listen from the inside in order to perceive the rightful course of action to undertake.

It is this inner way of knowingness that discloses to you a more joyful way of living. It softens the hard blows of disappointment and frustration that accompany everyday life. You were given many inner resources to help you navigate the conditions of your material life, yet you must use them appropriately in order to achieve the level of satisfaction you desire. All of the resources available to you grow commensurately with how persistently and wisely you use them. Come to me; ask your Mother to guide you to that place of understanding and you will learn how to use the wonderful resources of your mind and heart.

It is time to grow and mature as a child of the universe, my beloved. Learn to use your mind in the way that your Father and I have designed and planned, and all of what you need to live richly, fully, joyfully will be available to you!

"The resources available to you grow commensurately
with how persistently and wisely you use them."

Your Heart Has Strings that Vocalize the Song of Life

My little child, this is your Mother Spirit who speaks! Your human heart is a delicate and powerful instrument whose strings are designed to vocalize the song of life. My sounds of *joy* and *love* are the notes and chords your heart is designed to emit, and yet you sometimes close your heart because you feel pain or judgment. Do you not know, my beloveds, that it is *my* compassion that will ease the pain? Do you not recognize my desire to soothe your soul and thereby soften the blows of human suffering in your life?

When you ask for my sounds of love to emanate into another person's heartstrings, I ask you to pluck the notes of compassion and understanding for them. Allow that person's heart to communicate to yours what is needed. Then wait and ask me to send the notes and chords into them that will calm their mind and caress their heart.

As you begin to master your own heart and the energies you emit, you will help your brothers and sisters resonate with the love they desire and deserve. Together you compose a new song of the regenerative powers of creation. Sing these songs with all of the gusto you can muster, and allow my presence to thrive within you! Be in my joy!

New Circuits Will Make You Builders of a New Earth

Beloved child, your Mother is here for you! New circuits of Light and Life are now ready to intersect within and around you. Open yourself to these new particles of love and know that this is what was always intended for you to receive. My presence within your mind—your system of consciousness—has been designed to receive these new spiritual endowments, and only your desire is necessary for them to connect within you.

Sit now in your heart and ask for the celestial presences—those personalities who are able weave these circuits into your being—to come close to you and build you in this new circuitry of light. It is time for you to become more of what was always destined for you. Relax, breathe, and ask for them to come into your heart and mind. Trust, trust, trust that what is being shared with you is what you have long sought.

Child, stand tall in the presence of your own inner beauty and power. Claim your destiny as a child of love and Spirit. Know that your Father Michael and I are proud of our little ones now awakening to their true destinies, and that we are preparing you to be the healers and builders of the new Earth.

You Are Participating in the Unfolding of the Ages

Beloved child, this is your Mother of Spirit. As you grow into maturity, you enter the realm of adult spiritual development. An organic process slowly evolves you, both as an individual and as a member of society, into a perfect and balanced reflection of the divine. This is the unfolding of the ages, and your participation is most often unaware and unconscious.

Now, however, we are in a time of planetary transformation. You are being encouraged and trained to appreciate how much leeway and choice you have in the creation of your own perfection and balance. You are awakening to how your own uniqueness can contribute something special to the greater whole. You are also realizing that our desire to grow you into a mature, awakened person is not just something that benefits you; it also adds to the growing body of Christ Consciousness on the planet. We desire as your Parents to help you understand this basic cosmic responsibility to the whole. For our part, we provide you with a fertile environment so you can achieve this advanced state of being.

As you live each day, appreciate what it is you are doing by living and growing! You can enjoy the moments of every day by fully committing yourself to ripen like delicious fruit on a tree. Appreciate this natural process of maturing a little more each day, my child, and you will find the joy in life that makes this process exciting, creative, and a delight to all your senses.

"You are awakening to how your own uniqueness can contribute something special to the greater whole."

If You Get Stuck, Ask Me to Move You Forward

My beloved child, this is your Mother. These times of change can carry you into unchartered waters of life. Like a leaf flowing in a swift stream, you are sometimes carried by the pace of evolution into places where the water collects, and where you may feel like you are spinning around in a spiral but moving nowhere. You may feel stuck at this point, but in reality you are moving. It is just that your progress is not visibly moving you *forward* in that moment.

When you are at that place, just know that you need a gentle push to disengage you from the circling current. Here is where you can ask me as your Mother and Breath of Life to supply you with the momentum to propel you forward once again. But if you do so, you must be prepared for this change. For you will be taken to another place where you will learn new lessons and grow into new aspects of your spiritual nature. Sometimes this will feel uncomfortable at first, because what you are learning is unfamiliar. Be mindful as you go that such novel experiences take time to settle into your being and disclose what is important for you to understand. However, you are safe in these experiences because you are growing in *me*.

Trust in the flow of the waters of life, my child, for this is me sending you on your way. Trust that there is something innate within you that will guide you through this journey. Keep your heart open so you can more easily navigate around those inevitable eddies where you end up spinning around aimlessly. Remember that your personal desires are there to help you maneuver through the stagnant places where life seems pointless or discouraging. Know that you will discover in your heart the courage to move ahead and learn what your Indwelling Spirit wants to teach you about the ways of life. Be in my peace!

Open Your Heart to Your Universe Siblings

Beloved child, this is your Divine Mother. My being is radiating from the center of the universe to your hearts and minds. You are always in and with me, and I long for you to discover the secrets of my presence that will liberate you as the faith-sons and faith-daughters that you are. This is an inner journey that you take one step at a time, and each step brings you closer to me at the center of the cosmic home we share.

On your journey you will be introduced to many of your universe siblings, individuals who long to make your acquaintance and share with you their insights and wisdom. They have much to teach you to help you navigate this inner reality that is now opening in your heart and mind. Allow them to show you the way and to share their love with you. Trust me, my beloveds, and open your hearts to them.

Love is the language of the universe, and your elder brothers and sisters have much to share with you. Trust in me, trust in your Father, and trust in those who have your best interests at heart. Take time to sit in your heart and allow your brethren in Spirit to reach in and touch you with their compassion, concern, and care for you—for you are their younger brothers and sisters who are awakening to the grandeur of our family. Be in my peace!

"My being is radiating from the center of
the universe to your hearts and minds."

PART II

Messages of Truth from Our Divine Father

Our local universe Father is known on high as *Christ Michael*. He also is the divine personality who incarnated as Jesus and lived a human life on our world, *Urantia*. Along with our Divine Mother, he represents the eternal Trinity to our section of the evolving universe, which is known as *Nebadon* (see glossary). Michael is the source and the exemplar of every divine quality—love, compassion, understanding, forgiveness, peace, truth, goodness, beauty—and of all other traits we deem desirable and noble. Developing our relationship with him helps us receive his blessing and watchcare through the vehicle of his Spirit of Truth. He *is* the way, the truth, and the life.

"The nature of God can be best understood by the revelation of the Father which Michael of Nebadon unfolded in his manifold teachings and in his superb mortal life in the flesh."
—THE URANTIA BOOK

Now Is the Time to Reclaim Your Divine Inheritance

My beloved child, this is your Father. I am Michael, and I am known throughout the local universe as the Creator of this wonderful domain that you and I inhabit together. My Spirit Consort is your Divine Mother, and she and I are a co-creative unit. Long ago we left the eternal realms of Paradise to venture into time and space, creating our own home wherein many children of various orders and personality types are born, raised, live, and journey. You are a part of this vast organism of our universe, and you will reside here during your afterlife and for many ages to come as you become more spiritually oriented to the creation we all share.

It is my desire as your Creator Father that you to come into the fullness of your destiny. Your world has been quarantined from the rest of the universe for many years, yet you were always loved, wanted, and cherished. The spiritual circuits of your individual beings were always open to us, yet you knew us not because of the ways of men who wanted to keep you separated from us. This was a power struggle that perpetuated many lies about your nature and fostered religious dissension and disharmony among the peoples of your planet.

But now this is all being resolved. You, my child of this world, are awakening to the true call of your heart, and herein is where you will find what was once missing. Open to my Spirit of Truth within your beings, my beloved, and find the missing links that will fill you with hope, joy, forgiveness, compassion, peace, and love. Now is the time to reconnect, dear one, and reclaim your divine inheritance.

> "Your world has been quarantined from the rest of the universe for many years, yet you were always loved, wanted, and cherished."

Allow Me to Speak to Your Heart

Dear child, I am Michael, your Creator Father. Some of you may know me as "God" or as "Jesus"; others of you may sense me in your heart as "essence" or "source." I am here in whatever way you need me to be with you, for I love you with a strength and intensity that is beyond your ability to fully experience.

There is a connecting link within your being that ties us together in a holy union. This link is indissoluble, yet it becomes more present when you turn your sights inward to experience a reality that is, at the moment, much greater than you currently understand. Because of this growing connection between us, a current of spirit is now washing through you and bringing new life into your being. And part of that current contains information about me: who I am, what role I would like to play in your life, what relationship we can have together, and how I wish to draw very close to you.

What I ask of you is to hold open a place in your heart so I can speak into it. Ask questions of me: "Who are you, Michael?" "What is my relationship with you?" "Why should I have a relationship with you?" "What is the purpose of coming to know you?" Each question you pose to me in sincerity will be answered with love and compassion. I will speak the words you need to hear and I will fill your being with peace. I will hold you gently in my arms and help you feel safe. I will help you let go into my warmth of my being.

The life patterns on this world are changing rapidly, my child. More and more you need an anchor to hold you firm and stable during these times of tumultuous change and renewal. Sometimes the changes will affect you deeply and throw you off balance. That's why something must firmly be in place so you will not feel troubled by the circumstances of life at this time. One of my roles is to provide an anchor that brings peace and stability into your life. When you come to me sincerely asking for a relationship with me—no matter how large or small a presence you may want me to have in your life—I can secure you in my being. Renewal is yours for the asking.

A New Glory Will Blaze in the Hearts of All Humanity

Open your heart to me, my child, and sit in the beauty of my love for you. This is your Father; I am Michael, and I bid you greetings from the heavens. One day soon the veil between the worlds will be lifted and you will know your rightful place in the universe. The time is growing shorter when the separation between heaven and Earth will no longer be in place and when the glory that has been shrouded in secrecy, lies, greed, and blatant deception will blaze in the hearts of all humanity. This is my promise to you, little one, so I ask you to patiently await the time of your soul's liberation.

You can participate with me now in this liberation through your desire for heaven and Earth to conjoin. This is a heartfelt action you can take at any moment's notice, one that will give you a feeling of powerfulness and create new possibilities of self-actualization within you. As more spiritual power pours over the Earth, you will more perceptibly feel the truth in these words and more enthusiastically allow them to be the food that nourishes your soul.

When you see certain events unfolding before your eyes, place no thought of doubt or worry into them, assuming that no higher authority is acting on your behalf. I have made promises and commitments to this world. You can trust that all things are working toward the evolution of your planet to join the greater cosmic family. Trust in this alone, my child. Feel your desire for this reconnection to come about with glorious love; allow the deepest desires of your heart for the healing of all life on this world to occur. In doing so, you shall be adding your personal energy into the collective transformational force that is catalyzing these changes.

Together, you and I, universe child and Father, are building peace on Earth. In time, the rejoining of heaven and Earth will come to pass, and you will be delighted that you have participated in the most stupendous event this world has seen!

> "I have made promises and
> commitments to this world."

All Humanity Shall Awaken to the Truth

Beloved child, your Father speaks into your heart. Do you fully appreciate that you are my child and are entitled to receive a love so profound that it will change your life forever? Dare to dream and to imagine; soar into the limitless possibilities available to you. When you come to me, you are enlarging your sense of self into a realm of creative play where your inner potential blossoms, giving you much delight.

I, as your Father in Spirit, endow you with many wonderful and noble qualities that are all highly desirable for human growth and spiritual and intellectual development. As you come to me more and more in the awareness of our loving relationship, I will show you more of the beauteous parts of your being. Identifying with them will trigger new insights and allow more spiritual light to grow within you. This light that I now offer you is your soul's nourishment. Your old ideas and habits that have sabotaged your efforts to live righteously will gradually fade to nothing, the more you come to me.

The time is approaching when all people will know the truth of who they are and how vital they are to the universe. My children will know their worth and cast aside the tattered garments of isolation, fear, abandonment, guilt, and shame. You as my children are growing in power and might, and when the time is ripe, all shall awaken to the truth.

Live in this truth, my child, and you shall assist me in helping your slumbering brethren to awaken to their own glorious truth. Help me shorten the days of darkness. Help me to remove the veils that have separated your world from truth. Come into me, live in me, and you shall obtain everything your heart desires, even the highest dreams of your imagination!

> "Help me to remove the veils that have separated your world from truth."

Usher in the New Dawn by Centering Yourself in Me

Arise, my child, and usher in the new age that is dawning upon Urantia! The time is upon us when my truth shall ring in the hearts of all humanity—the good news that *all* people on Earth are beloved of the Father and are now being uplifted into the greater family of the cosmos.

Let your hearts stir with my words of comfort and hope and know that you are being made anew in Spirit. This renewal will bring forth an unfolding of great beauty in your own life and in the everyday lives of your brothers and sisters. The harvest is upon us, and the time is now to step out in faith and bring my children to me.

I have spoken these words through many. And now I wish to once again convey my desire that all people come into my bosom and receive the divine comfort that heals the human heart of its many afflictions. If you receive me in this way—and if you provide more space for me within your own heart—my children will come to know me through you.

Go deeper now, inside your heart. Feel my heart beating within yours and know that I sit and wait for you. Through your beating heart will you know my presence, my child. Once you center yourself in me, I am able to speak the comforting words that you as my child need to hear. And as you become a mouthpiece of Spirit, the loving words you lend to my children will uplift them into my embrace, where they will be healed.

Therefore, come to me more and more each day. Feel me in your beating heart and I will speak more resoundingly to you. The truth is alive inside of you. Feel it! Desire this! It is time to cast aside all shadows of the past. I am the Truth and the Light. Live in me and know the joys of living. Pass this on to your brothers and sisters in as many ways as you can as we journey to the Paradise Father together. Life is joyous, and wonder is all around you. I leave you in my peace wrapped in the arms of your Mother, who carries my Spirit through your mind and body. I am Michael.

Become More Responsible for and Responsive to Love

My child, this is your Father in Spirit. While your world grows in my spirit luminosity, know that you have certain responsibilities in relation to this energetic presence of truth, goodness, and beauty. You are responsible to receive in your own heart this new presence of love. Allow this energy to grow and become the most powerful force within your being.

How open you will be to this spiritual presence is up to you, my child. I, as your Creator Father, make it available for your healing and upliftment; it is your choice whether or not you will receive it. The time is upon your world to decide whether or not to embrace what is being offered to you. Many hungry hearts know not the simplicity of going within to receive their divine birthright, where they can experience that all-pervading sense of loving acceptance as my child.

So it becomes a matter of encouraging those of you who *do* have an open heart to open it ever wider and deeper. Then you will receive a love that renews itself the more you give it away to others. Therefore, as you receive my love, offer it to your starving brothers and sisters. Imbibe deeply of my Spirit Presence that I may continue to renew you. And then, give it out to others through the magnetic presence in your heart that draws others to you for refreshment. Allow yourself to become more responsible and responsive to receiving love.

Love as I love, my child, give as I give, share as I share, and you will have provided yourself an ever-renewing wellspring of all the love you need to find the security, happiness, and joy that life can bring to you.

"As you receive my love, offer it to
your starving brothers and sisters."

Your Planet is Opening Its Doors to the Universe

My beloved child, this is your Father Michael. The call for truth within your heart is resounding and getting stronger each day. For many eons you have been shielded from the knowledge of your planet's history and the long drama that prevented you from fully accepting your divine inheritance. But the time of truth is now upon you, my children. It is my delight to open the heavens to bring you that which you most long to know: who you are in the vast starry cosmos of the universe.

You are my child who is living in my universe home. This is your domicile for many millennia while you gain experience and understanding of the natural workings of creation. You live on a planet that struck out on its own, essentially casting aside the divine plans of our Creator; and it is now reaping what was sown so long ago. You are hardly aware of the synchronistic orchestration of this vast domain and how its operations contribute to the greater good and well-being of all inhabitants, not just a select few. Your planet is now opening its doors to the universe, so that my ways and my truth may reveal your place in the home I have prepared for you.

The universe is alive and waiting to show you its wonders and joys. Open your heart that you may enjoy what is yours to explore. Here in your heart is where you will find me, and where you will find your own creation story—the gift of the Father's love for you that sent you forth into the cosmos to explore the full spectrum of life, from human to divine. Allow your heart to open to the song of creation living within it, and you shall rejoice in the wonder of life!

> "You live on a planet that struck out on its own,
> essentially casting aside the divine plans of our Creator;
> and it is now reaping what was sown so long ago."

As Your Father I Give You What You Need

My child, listen to my words of encouragement throughout the day. You need reassurance that all is well within as you undergo many changes. I will speak to you in your heart when you focus on me and ask for my words to uplift you.

As your Father, I know what you need. When you are aware of a pressing urgency that weighs upon your soul, never hesitate to come to me and ask me to fill you with something good and love-filled; as your Source I will feed you and acknowledge that urgency. Remember, I give you what you need! This is my long-awaited opportunity to help you realize who you are.

Staying close to me during your day will make you more effective in all areas of your life. You will find that you are less self-absorbed because you will feel more secure and confident in who you are. This tendency toward self-forgetfulness allows you to manifest your beauty in the world, thus creating more light for others to see.

Ignite the light within by focusing on me in the small moments in your life. Each time you do this the light will grow brighter. Each time you remember who you are, you will offer someone else the opportunity for their Spirit to help them remember who they are. Let yourself be a manifestation of love. As my words of encouragement build you in the foundation of love, know that you are bringing more of this divine substance to your world. The ways of spirit are lovingly restoring beauty, grace, and charm to all.

Say "Yes" to Me Frequently Each Day

Dearest child, this is your Father. I am Michael. Like the days of spring when the hours of daylight are lengthened, so too are the energies of Spirit expanding themselves in length and breadth on this world. Rejoice! Love is gaining strength and expression here, and you can rest in the assurance that all is occurring as it should.

As the protector of your world, I hold a place in my heart for this planet to be uplifted into the energy of light and into the saving grace of love. You can assist me in bringing more love into this world by opening your heart even more to me—by saying "yes" to me as your Father as I attempt to communicate with you during your day.

In saying "yes" you are claiming more of who you are; you receive more fibers of light into your body; you infuse yourself with more love—the energy that pierces through all pain and suffering and releases you from all fear. Say "yes" to me more often during your day by reciting these words in your heart: "Not my will but *yours* be done in me, Father!" You never know what gifts I will give you when you say this to me.

I invite you to do this as frequently as you can during your day, my child. You honor yourself in doing so. You also honor your brothers and sisters who need the light of love in their life as you build more love-energy onto the planet. In time you will recognize that saying "yes" to me is your greatest duty as a child of Spirit and your greatest joy. I give you all things to renew you and the world. Will you do your part to receive these gifts and share them with others?

Enter the Journey of the Heart and Discover the Universe

My child, this is your Father Michael. There is a path that leads you into a garden of light and laughter—the very realm of glory and goodness. This image is no fairy tale for the young, but a story of adventure for the young at heart. Do you want to venture out on this journey?

This journey of the heart takes you on the inner path to find out who you truly are. You get to investigate the myriad dimensions of self and to increasingly see yourself as you are: a budding spirit growing on a physical world. How beautiful and tender is the young spiritual creation that you are. See yourself in this light and feel the splendor at your core!

Your inner journey will uncover many new ideas to consider about yourself and your reality. It will expand your awareness of the rich layers of the universe, and bring you into a new understanding of what life is. The questions pressing upon your soul will be answered; the longings of your heart will be satisfied.

Allow me to open the door for you by asking me to open your heart. As your Spirit Father I can do this for you. You are safe and secure with me. It is time: open your heart and discover the universe!

Accept Yourself Completely, Just As You Are

Child of the light, come to your Father of Lights. I am Michael, and I receive you in the fullness of your humanness. Bare your souls to me and I will show you how precious and beloved you are.

The day is dawning when humanity will know its full worth. Gone will be the days of discarded lives, abandoned hopes, destroyed dreams. I open the portals of love more fully when you are ready to see yourselves as I see you. When you can accept yourself *just as you are*, then will my love pour into every cell and make you more than you are now.

The great quest for the completion of self is underway as each man, woman, and child of this world receives the flow of my love into their being. Whether here on this world or the next, my children will come to know and appreciate their value. What a joyous day that will be when my children fall in love with their true selves and honor what my Father in Paradise has spread out before them—the ascension path to glory!

I prepare your way, and I will show you how to walk this path in joy and lightheartedness. Come to me, my child, as we walk together to the Source and luxuriate in the grandeur of All That Is.

"Bare your souls to me and I will show
you how precious and beloved you are."

Learn to Identify With Your Soul

My dear child, this is your Father Michael, and I welcome you to join me in celebrating yourself! Your self-image is something that is constantly changing as your life experiences take you into unknown places. Sometimes you will feel weak and small; sometimes you will feel more confident and secure. Regardless of how you perceive yourself, know that you are deeply loved by your Mother and me, and that you are valuable and important to the fabric of reality.

I encourage you to see yourself as we, your Parents in Spirit, see you. There is a quiet objectivity that we can impart to you that helps you to see yourself with more compassion and humor. This perspective on yourself is vital to your growth, as it builds a light-hearted feeling within your body.

You were designed to grow step by step, decision by decision, experience by experience. You have been given a spirit-pilot to guide you so that you stay true to your innate nature. Your natural being is indeed a joy to behold. It is quite wondrous for us to watch as you become more aware of who you truly are. The image of self you now hold is primarily something that you have inherited through your cultural conditioning; but the image of your *soul* is what truly discloses your current status and your divine nature.

I invite you to discover your soul-image and I ask you to see and claim it as your true identity. Then you can allow the streams of heaven's love to magnetize you homeward to your eventual destination. Will you open yourself to your soul, my beloved one? Only then will you find the fire to ignite your passion to live more gloriously and harmoniously within the will of Spirit, in whose image you were made.

A New Foundation Is Opening Within You

My child, this is Michael, the Father of your universe. Your Spirit Mother and I welcome you into our larger universe of which you are an integral part. A new reality is now being opened to you; we are offering you bigger conceptual frames of reference for understanding who you are, your relationships, your social institutions, your planet, even the universe. With this new foundation, we invite you to question everything: what is real, what upholds your life, what gives you a sense of purpose. All this is possible because you are moving from the old support system of your culture into a deeper reliance on your inner foundation, now rooted in Spirit, from which the divine principles of life originate—truth, goodness and beauty.

As your foundation opens further, you will naturally scrutinize the belief systems in your culture. During this season of change, let go of your attachments to the human-made institutions crumbling before you. Instead, look again to the inner foundation expanding within your hearts and minds. You are being transformed internally, slowly but surely. However, you do have command of this process by your willingness to participate with the liberating action of the Spirit within you. We simply ask you to trust in your Spirit to give you what you need as your foundation is increasingly infused with truth and goodness.

Let all of this be a sorting process. As your inner foundation is renewed in Spirit, you will find that you more naturally gravitate toward positive actions because you feel and think in a more divinely inspired way. As you grow in this dynamic, we will strengthen this foundational structure of consciousness so that you grow ever more in harmony with the divine ways of life.

You Are Safe in Me Despite the Chaos and Turmoil

Beloved one, this is your Spiritual Father, who greets you with open arms and a loving heart. Be at peace; you are safe. Although the winds of change whirl all around you, you are indeed protected because you live in me.

I understand how you perceive your life's situation. What you see before you colors how you feel and think. Yet, if you were to turn to me at a moment's notice, I could give you better ideas of how to consider your current reality. Let not what you see with your physical eyes cause you to doubt the reality of my existence within you.

The world is fraught with chaos and turmoil and will continue to be so for a time to come. You, however, can find ultimate and lasting peace by coming to me and nestling yourself in my bosom. There you will find rest and respite, and you will feel protected. The outer circumstances of your life may change, but your inner reality will be anchored in a serenity that no one can ever take from you.

I am your Father and I love you deeply. Envision strong, loving arms enfolding you and holding you close. Ask for my love to flow from my heart into yours. Feel a strong warmth and a steady pulse move through your being. This is *me*, your Spirit Father, coursing through your body and mind, bringing you the comfort and fulfillment you require for your spiritual growth.

I gave you life that you might have it abundantly. Take it. It is yours, my beloved child! Come to me and receive.

> "I gave you life that you
> might have it abundantly."

Open Now to Life Eternal and Abundant

I am Michael. I am the Father of the universe of your habitation. In coming to know who I am, you are opening the door to the essential adventure of life! It is from me that you *have* life, and it is *in* me that your being comes into its fullest dimension as a child of Spirit.

Just as your human father contributed to your human nature, so do I contribute to your divine or higher nature. Your spiritual heredity is indissolubly linked to me, and I feed the qualities of Spirit into you through your Divine Mother—in whose universe womb you grow. Begin now to think of yourself more as *our* offspring rather than as the child of human parents, and you will begin to accept more of your divine nature and embody it more fully.

You have been deprived of so much because you live on a world plagued with wars and poverty, illness and strife. Yet in me is *life*—eternal and abundant—and knowing this truth is your salvation from all of the challenges of daily living. Renew yourself each day by coming to me and asking for my living essence to feed you. Still your mind by taking yourself away from your day of busyness. Ask me to replenish your mind and body.

Grow each day in me, and I will indeed show you who you are. Little by little will you come into your higher self, whose internal light will glow outwardly more and more. Soon you will become more fully enmeshed in a radiant garment of light as my Spirit pours forth from your being. Then, you will be the living light of truth walking in human form on Earth. Then, you will be the vehicle for me to heal the wounds of this world. Then, you and I will collaborate to create heaven on Earth!

Allow Me to Mold You as Your Master Potter

My beloved child, your Father Michael greets you! Striving to attain new experiences is innate to being human. You have a natural "program" living inside each cell that compels you into action. You were meant to live dynamic, interesting, explorative lives that bring out the best in you. And you are designed to take your raw humanness and craft it into a work of art.

But the challenges of self-perfection were not meant for you to handle on your own. Your Mother and I created you, and therefore we can help you build a strong, noble, and gracious character. Work with us as we graft the seeds of your divine nature into your raw human self. Use these seeds and develop them into blossoms—through your daily actions and your relationships with others.

Allow yourself to be like clay in my hands. I am the master potter who can help mold you into a beautiful vessel of Spirit. Rest yourself in my hands and I will shape you according to the plans you contain within your being. I know your nature and your being thoroughly. I know where the rough stubs are on your vessel; I know where the smooth and lovely places are.

Trust your being to my artistry and we will make you more beautiful than you can imagine!

"I will shape you according to the
plans you contain within your being."

Fulfill Your Spiritual Needs by Asking for Our Support

Beloved child, this is your Father. I am Michael. What you do with your day is, of course, up to you. You all have work to do to maintain your material existence. But what do you do each day to maintain your *spiritual* existence? This is up to you as well. Equally as important as your material needs are your spiritual needs. For example, how much love do you need each day to be fulfilled? How much peace, how much patience, how much tolerance, how much understanding of others? These are real needs, my child, and I ask you to look at each one more carefully.

What will you do each day to meet your spiritual needs to your satisfaction? The attempts you make to still your mind and to spend quiet moments in reflection, prayer, and meditation— asking for your spirit to be replenished—are what will satisfy your spiritual longings. Remember that this practice is a vital part of your life; be sure to always spend some time coming to your Mother and me for our support. We will fill you with what you need spiritually.

You have so many choices to make during the day about how you fill your mental space. Cultivate a higher standard of spiritual living by focusing on the qualities of Spirit—which are always available to you at any moment's notice—by focusing inwardly and asking for them. You can still go about your daily tasks in your outer life, yet your inner life can be pointed in our direction. Aim your thoughts toward us when you have a need. This will give you an enduring stability that will center you in the present moment.

We are in you always, children, yet you become *aware* of us by turning your thoughts over to us through your desire for contact—which is your conscious choice. Will you give us more permission to bring you the good things of Spirit by asking for them throughout your day? Pose this question to yourself over and over and see what results you get!

Prepare for the Turmoil Ahead by Receiving My Love

My beloved child, this is your Father. I am Michael. Surround yourself in the love of friends and family, as well as those beings who serve you yet remain unseen. This blanket of love is your protection against those cold, harsh realities of the turmoil of change on this world. Keep yourselves close to love and you will be safe.

Think not that the ways of the past will leave this planet without a struggle. Envision yourselves as being in the midst of a storm, yet safely placed within its eye where peace and stability keep you protected. Here is where you find me holding you steadfastly in my arms as I witness with you what is happening on your world. With me, you will be able to view the coming changes as positive and necessary. They allow new things to take root and grow in a purified soil of love, peace, understanding, compassion, and forgiveness. And these qualities will actually grow out of the residues of poverty, greed, hate, war, anger, and destruction. All of this is occurring now as my essence pours over this world.

Prepare yourselves for more change by allowing those deepest places of your inner being to come before me. Expose yourselves more fully to me, my beloved, and you will be given so much love and peace that you won't know what to do with it all! Your destiny is to live in this love forever. Even though your body contains resistance to experiencing me fully in each cell, by coming to me with your willingness to be a full vessel of my love, you will continually receive and absorb it until you are fully sated in this most glorious and wondrous of energies.

Now is your time for healing and recovery—for discovering your true self that was seeded within your being from the beginning. I yearn to help you into this new fabric of life, my child. I long to hold this garment in front of you to step into, and to watch your eyes as your amazement unfolds, as you settle yourself into your new *persona*. Change is wonderful, my children; the changes to come will bring you closer to me.

Open to Me—I Am Your Source of Spirit

My child, this is your Father Michael. I am a great spiritual power in your life, and when you allow me to come into your mind and body, I bring into you something dynamic and uplifting. I bring you *Spirit*, which is the very essence of love and goodness, and of truth and beauty; it is also the substance your body and mind require to grow strong and healthy.

In truth, you cannot live without Spirit because you are an essential part of it. You were designed to understand who and what Spirit is, why Spirit is vital, and how to *become* Spirit. I will speak into your heart about these things when you come to me and simply ask questions.

I *am* Spirit. I am your Source of Spirit, and I invite you to come to know who I am and what role I play in your life. This invitation is always open to you when you are ready. I will satisfy every longing of your soul and set you on the path to fulfillment beyond your wildest imaginings, for you are my dearly beloved child.

> "I bring you *Spirit*, which is the very essence
> of love and goodness, and of truth and beauty."

Ponder the True Cost of Spiritual Growth

Greetings, my child! This is your Creator Father. I ask you, what is the cost of growing spiritually? What is the price of becoming more spirit-like? Ponder these questions and challenge yourself, with honesty and sincerity, to look inside for answers.

You live in a culture that is dominated by the idea of cost: if something is valuable, then a price must be paid to acquire it. In keeping with this train of thought, ask yourself what outlay is required of you in order to develop the spiritual side of your nature. What will your life become like if you open to a higher part of yourself? Does growing up spiritually mean you must give up certain material possessions or particular relationships? How does it feel inside to live a genuinely spiritual life? Do you sense fear or resistance? Or do you experience elation or joy? Reflecting on such questions is part of the process of determining the true value of spiritual development.

I will be with you in Spirit as you ask yourself these questions. Come into my presence and ask, and I will reveal to you the truth about the real cost of your growth.

Serve Others As and Where They Are

My child, your Father Michael greets you. I call you into the sacred service of helping your brothers and sisters into their divine inheritance. While you are not responsible for their awakening, I encourage you to help them grow into a new self-awareness through your loving compassion, and to do so regardless of their status. Love your brothers and sisters exactly where they are, knowing that they too are on their journey. Perhaps they are not as far along as you are; nevertheless, they are seeking and they are on their own path.

It is challenging to meet each individual right where they are on the path they have chosen. When you minister to this person, you do not have to be concerned about the words you speak. Allow me to speak for you. Simply sit in your heart center and hold the intention and desire for my words to resonate into their soul. The more you can focus on this intention, the more you will be able to *let go* and allow me to guide the person before you. In this manner you allow the pressure you may have placed upon yourself to be released, freeing my words to echo in their hearts.

By following this approach, service becomes easier and more inspired, and you learn how to better connect with your Mother and me. You discover how to listen with your heart to another person's journey, thereby validating them. Plus, you provide a safe space for them to trust you as you focus on their needs. You feel spiritual energy moving as it connects you together, and you forge a real bond. What's more, the effects in your body are pleasurable and healing.

My children, if you could only feel a measurement of the good you do when you allow yourselves to be available for service, you would be serving all day long! So, become more mindful of the opportunities before you. Open your hearts with the desire to be of service to me, your Mother, and the universe, and allow us to surprise you with new brothers and sisters to love!

Have Trust in the Goodness of Unselfishness

My beloved child, this is your Father Michael. When you arise each day, focus on your Spirit within for a few moments. Give thanks that you are ready to live another day and that you will have many opportunities during the day to be of help to your brothers and sisters. Of course, there are many ways you can show them your love: a simple smile, a helpful hand with a chore, compassionate listening, or volunteering your time for social causes. The opportunities for you to share your love are boundless; how you share your love is *your* choice.

As you shift your awareness to your Inner Voice, you will notice that you become less self-centered and more attentive to the needs of others. Such a shift discloses an important new phase in your growth. It signifies that you are now moving away from the needs of self and becoming more service-oriented, where you will find more freedom in the Spirit. This liberated state of mind provides you with greater joy and helps you face your daily existence with more hope and faith. Further, this attitude keeps the flow of spiritual energy moving through you, which in turn gives you a deeper sense of belonging to us as your Divine Parents.

Learn to trust in the goodness of unselfishness when it is motivated by mercy and compassion. Life becomes more grace-filled when you carry this love around you as you go about your day. Others will sense this, and you will naturally be drawn to sharing your love in the small or large ways that intuitively feel right to you.

> "As you shift your awareness to
> your Inner Voice, you will notice
> that you become less self-centered."

The Times Ahead Will Be the Thrill of Your Mortal Life

My love overshadows this world, my child. You are being bathed in light as each cell begins to ingest higher energies that have not been available heretofore on this world. Drink in this energy and breathe it in; savor its presence. You are being called into a higher form of love as my divine embrace enfolds your beautiful planet.

Yes, there is a challenging period ahead that will test you and prepare you for higher expressions of service to your brothers and sisters in need. I encourage you to look at these times as the thrill of a mortal lifetime. You are being given many wonderful opportunities to test your mettle and see exactly what you are made of. So, engage boldly with what your planet is undergoing, so that your brothers and sisters may witness spirit in action.

Know that you walk with me and that I am with you always. I hold your hand; I know where the pitfalls are and I will keep you safe on the path. Trust me. Trust me. Trust me. You will need to remember this as your world changes around you and the times of tumult seem to engulf the planet. Know that this turmoil is only transitory. It will pass.

I am the peace of the ages. I am the caretaker of all. This world shall be born anew and all things renewed in Spirit. I am Michael, and I am your Father. Live in me and your hearts shall rejoice in what is being birthed through the womb of your Mother as you come into the embrace of our universal family!

In the Midst of Conflict, Focus on Me as Your Center

My children, this is your Father Michael. Conflicts between people and their belief systems will challenge you for many years to come. These times of planetary change will help you understand that conflict is innate to the human struggle to attain divinity. When you are in the midst of conflict, focus on me as your center and I will help you through the storm. Hold fast onto your thoughts of me as you ride it out. Then, look back upon the conflict and ask yourself these questions:

- What just happened?
- Why did it happen?
- What did I do to contribute to the conflict?
- What was the other person's role in the conflict?
- What is the spiritual approach to resolution?

Spend time in stillness and allow the Spirit Within to sort out the truth so you can perceive with more objectivity what has occurred. I realize this approach will take time and practice. Yet, if you can carry it out, you will add a deeper pool of understanding, compassion, and insight to your soul's growth.

Again, this is truly a challenging time for the humans of this world. You are facing major conflicts in all areas of your life, yet there *will* be resolution on your world and, finally, peace. Stay anchored in me and I will help you attain the harmony you seek—provided you take the necessary measures of self-responsibility that I recommend, which in turn will afford you with deeper insight into any situation that has been fraught with conflict.

> "Conflict is innate to the human
> struggle to attain divinity."

Build Your Dreams of Hope in Me

Come into me, my child. This is your Father. I am Michael. Look not to the ways of the world to make sense of the future of humanity. I hold the plans for the evolution of this world in my hands, and so I say to you: build your dreams of hope in *me*.

As you and your world undergo seemingly radical shifts in perceptions and cultural changes, what will you use as your anchor to keep yourself emotionally stable and secure? Where will you choose to put your faith and hope? How will you help your family and friends make sense of the changes they are encountering in their lives?

Peace does not come easily to the human mind, yet it is well within reach. It is within you, and it is I who infuse the qualities of assurance, calm, and patience into you. *Come to me*. Focus on me and ask me to fill you with peace during these times of personal and planetary turbulence. I can indeed put your mind to rest about what is occurring all around you. Will you invite me in so I may give you a greater perspective of what is happening? Will you trust me that all things work for the good and glory of Spirit? Will you stand fast in me while I build a new planetary culture with your hands doing the work?

I am here to anchor in a new light and truth on Earth. I can only do this when your heart and hands are stabilized by me. If you allow your doubt to yield to my will and my love, you will receive the peace you require to keep you secure. Together, you and I will build this world into a place of beauty and goodness where justice, fairness, equality, peace, and freedom are available to all men, women, and children everywhere. Will you come to me now and allow this to happen?

Allow Me to Reveal What a True Father Is

My child, this is your Father Michael. You may have wondered: What is a father? What does being a father mean? Look to me to discover the ways of fatherliness! Sadly, so many of my children of this world have been hurt terribly by their human fathers. They have either turned away from them entirely, or else they have not been able to enjoy a loving relationship with them. However, when you come to me in trust, I will reveal my loving nature to you. I will help you overcome those experiences from childhood and beyond that removed from your divine inheritance the experience of being valued as children of God.

Words cannot adequately express what being a father is. The characteristics of patience, understanding, appreciation, kindness, and compassion are some of what you may understand to comprise noble human behavior. But being a father is something even more. You experience the true qualities of fatherliness whenever you receive what I—as your divine Father—can uniquely provide for you, especially when you step up and ask to receive it. Then I will imprint upon you what a true Father provides. Coming to me repeatedly in this way will help you validate your innate being as a child of God, and you will begin to sense how intrinsic you are to the whole universe. But this confirmation of your value cannot be taught—it must be experienced. As you amass these experiences, your understanding grows and begins to register upon your being just who your Father is and what fatherliness is.

When you come to me as your "Dad" I will validate you in my love. I will help you build upon your innate need to be acknowledged as having a right to exist. Come to me, now, my beloved. Sit in the quiet of your heart and I will speak my love into you!

> "I will imprint upon you
> what a true father provides."

Let Yourself Be Infused by the Language of Creation

Beloved one, this is your Father Michael. Come to me and let me share with you in the joys of your human experience! Now is the time to cast off the shadows of fear and doubt that have affected your ability to live in creativity and love. Now is the time to open your hearts and breathe in the wonder of life all around you. As you do so, allow your Mother to infuse you with the language of *Creation*.

This is a powerful language that discloses all that you need to live and thrive, my children. This is a part of your divine birthright, and we are here to help you become infused with its ability to shift your internal structure to help you embrace more of who you truly are. Sit, breathe, and invite into your being this word "Creation" that contains dynamic information. Breathe and relax as you allow it to descend upon you and vibrate within your being.

Invite your Mother to send her life-giving Breath of Life into your heart, into your lungs, into your cells, into your whole body. Release any tension and give it to me. Send it on its way! Embrace her energies of Creation with a full heart now, and you will receive what you need.

Do this each day, my children, and allow the living languages that are entering you to play at changing your inner structure. *Be* in this meditative space as much as you need to, and each day grow a little more divinely beautiful in the image of your *Creator*.

Receive from Me the Noble Traits You Desire

My child, this is your Father Michael. Come into my heart and receive those traits you value as worthy and noble. In me you will receive compassion, tolerance, patience, trust, kindness, understanding, and peace.

The divine attributes are real; they are part of the deities that created the universe. And all of these attributes that you desire are contained in *me*. Come to me, my children, that you each may receive what you need each day to become more Godlike in your own unique way.

With each breath you take with the intention to become Godlike you drink in my presence. You expand into the light of life that helps you stay healthy and positive. You even create those pathways that your cellular mechanisms require. You become more divinely real.

The nobility of being human is in striving to perfect yourself by your motivations to become more Godlike. You may fall short of your daily expectations. But know that when you enter into and rest in my heart, you will receive what I wish to share with you. Gain strength here, my children, and know that what you are becoming each day brings you closer to what your heart truly desires.

"The nobility of being human is in striving to perfect yourself by your motivations to become more Godlike."

Ask for My Trustworthiness to Fill You

My beloved child, this is your Father Michael. Trustworthiness is a quality of my personality that I share with you to help you gain greater confidence in the operations of the universe. This is important because you live on a world that has deviated from the divine plan, and you have been taught many erroneous ideas of who and what God is. One of the most helpful ways to overcome those old concepts is to sit in the quiet of your heart and to ask for *trustworthiness* to fill you. This new inner reality will offset the mistrust that you feel because the ways of the world and as a result of those individuals who have betrayed or hurt you.

Trust is a very important dimension of Spirit that will help you through planetary changes that will seem to be chaotic. I am here to walk with you through these transitional times, but you need to *trust* me. The old beliefs and other thought forms lodged within your being may seem to thwart your ability to trust me, but when you ask for *trustworthiness* and *trust* to fill your heart, I will respond.

So, my beloved, move beyond the pain of this world that keeps you in fear or confusion. Ask me to build this trust foundation in you to keep you in my peace as you walk into the new planetary culture being built upon your world. I am here for you, even if it seems that all is crumbling around you. I will strengthen and uphold you and keep you steady in forgiveness, patience, love, compassion and, above all, a peace that will astonish you and delight you! Grow in my *trustworthiness*!

Your Desire for Change Helps Us Transform the World

Beloved child, this is your Universe Father. In these times of transition, we encourage you to *expand* your dreams that love and peace reign supreme on Urantia. If you offer us these heart energies, my child, we will weave them into the expanding consciousness of love on your world so that they take root in the planetary web of consciousness. You can do your part each day by focusing on your desires for a new world.

Through your aspiration for change, you provide the mental and emotional environment needed for us to help you grow in love. Your desires are of utmost importance to us, for they serve as the catalyst for all good change to occur. You are powerful conductors of desires when they are focused in the *will of Spirit*. When you hold that focus, you will benefit greatly as you continue to align your hearts with ours.

Therefore, take your heart-power and learn to use it appropriately and wisely. The world is waiting for this, my beloveds, and you are the ones who are creating it as you learn to focus in your hearts, from your hearts, and through your hearts. Practice this more faithfully each day, and watch with wonderment how Spirit moves in and through you! Be in my peace!

"Your desires are of utmost importance
to us, for they serve as the catalyst
for all good change to occur."

Make Your Spiritual Growth Your Utmost Priority

Beloved child, this is your Father Michael. I want you to know that your spiritual growth is your most prized possession. No one can take this from you, because it is the single area of your life where you have ultimate control. How will you treat this possession? How will you make use of your capacity to grow in Spirit? Ultimately, these are the deepest and most meaningful questions a person can ask, and I ask you to ponder them now.

I am your elder brother Jesus who lived a human life on this world. I well understand the challenges of growing on such a sphere where the light of truth has been dimmed. Yet within your being is your own inner light that wants to shine brightly and to bring you the joyful serenity that comes from the connection to your Divine Source. It is the goal of human life to merge into this light, to become *one* with the light within. Have you made this the utmost priority of your life?

I ask these questions for you to think about more consistently throughout your day. Your world will be making some great changes in how it operates, and I desire that you are able to see yourselves through this time with hope, courage, patience, and joy. Remember that you have in me both a divine Father and a human brother. I can share with you those inner resources that will stimulate your spiritual growth and accompany you through this time. You never walk alone as you grow—and yet it is *you* who must take this journey to become that which is in your heart to express.

So be of good cheer, my children, as the light of truth grows upon our world. Rejoice in your ability to grow spiritually! Trust in what is happening to you internally—that more lights are indeed turning on within your being, and the universe is responding with its love, compassion, and devotion to help you grow in grace and beauty. Make the most of these gifts each day, and you shall surely flourish in the ways of Spirit.

Allow Me to Melt the Walls of Your Heart

Come, my child, and be with me. I am your Father, Michael, and I cherish you with an affection so tender and gentle that you can safely walk into my arms with delight and glee!

Too often my children of this world think they suffer on their own, when in reality I walk invisibly beside them. Still, you do not notice me. Your heart has not felt my presence inside you, closed off as it is. Feelings of defensiveness and abandonment sometimes make impenetrable walls in the heart vessel, but if you were to trust me more implicitly I would melt these walls down with my caress.

I know you inside and out. I know the pain you hold. Give it *all* to me and I will renew you with an energy so sweet that you will be surprised with wonderment as to why you held on to the pain at all. Let every memory contained in your body that does not serve you become *mine*. Turn it all over to me, and be innocent and fresh once more!

This is the promise I make to you, my child, simply because I love you. I created you and you are mine. Come to me more frequently with your requests for renewal, and allow me to show you the love you have always wanted.

"Too often my children of this world think
they suffer on their own, when in reality
I walk invisibly beside them."

Show the Way Forward for Your Suffering Brethren

Beloved child, this is your Father Michael. Growing up to be strong in Spirit will take you into life situations where your integrity is tested. How will you respond in these situations when confronted with the pain and suffering of your brethren? Will you succumb to their levels of despair? Or will you encourage them and lend them a helping hand to rise above their anguish? Will you help them recognize that their current dilemma is but a fleeting shadow of what is true, enduring, and uplifting?

I know you face many struggles in your civilizations as the seeming problems of the world mount. Yet I encourage you to look past what you see. Instead, know within your hearts that these difficult times are just the last vestiges of a way of living that is being removed from your planetary consciousness. You, as a body of collective humanity, are learning just how destructive certain mindsets are and how they damage human happiness and the well-being of the planet. Those who are pursuing such a destructive course are now becoming more visible in relation to everyone else. This polarization will compel the people of the world to look in a different direction. Meanwhile, you whose lives are transforming are the ones who will act as signals and signs for your brethren to also change course.

So, here I stand, drawing you into my presence. As you come to me, you will find the strength to withstand the storms of change that course through the social order of civilization. Come into my *peace*, my *comfort*, my *strength*, my *understanding*, and my *love* to carry you through this transition period, trusting in the *goodness* and *mercy* of our care as we help you build a new planetary reality.

Know That Chaos Eventually Leads to Order

My beloved child, this is Michael. Chaos always leads to order in the universe. There are times when activities seem to be destructive and disorganized, yet there is a purpose to this. Eventually, these occurrences will serve to eliminate that which is misaligned in the will of the Father. This is indeed what is happening on Urantia at the present time, and all of you are affected to various degrees by what is presently underway. Many of you will feel unsettled, confused, and even fearful.

Chaos within your being, however, is capable of being soothed and brought into order. Enter the quiet of your mind and ask your Mother and me to bring you into *peace*, *security*, and *safety*. Sit in stillness and receive what you need. You will then emerge refreshed with this energy and experience a higher level of serenity that you can then take with you out into the world. Anchor yourselves in us, my children, and allow our presence to emerge larger in scope within and around you.

Again I ask, how will you respond to this pivotal moment in your planet's history? You have choices to make each day. We will feed you with ideas to consider and feelings that will support you in facing your world. Choose your thoughts and actions carefully, my child. Bring your own internal chaos into order and increasingly master the vehicle you were given to live in. Be in my peace!

I Will Bind Up the Broken Hearts of My Children

My beloved child, your Father Michael greets you this day! Turbulent times of change are coming to Urantia, but fear not! I am with you always, and I will bind up the broken hearts of my children. I will deliver them into a new reality of *love, peace, compassion, mercy, and understanding.* As you comprehend these words in your mind and contemplate their meaning in your soul, doubt not that I am holding you securely in my being. Having once been a human among you, I know well what you are going through. Neglect not to call upon me as you witness what is now unfolding.

You see, my child, things that do not serve the evolution of the universe will not stand the test of time. What your world is undergoing is a rather rapid shift in consciousness, unlike anything seen in all of Nebadon, your universe home. I am ushering in the new era of Spirit. I am here to support your yearning for Godlikeness and your desire to learn, grow, and achieve that state of Christ consciousness that is yours for the striving.

The ways of heaven are upon you. This is a special time of divine grace, when the Father Creator of all is building the way of Spirit upon this Earth. Therefore, allow the will of creation to move into and through you, building in you the new reality of life. These are the glory times, my child, and the eyes of your celestial brothers and sisters are now upon you. They send their love and support to you so that you may ascend into the light that is your divine birthright.

> "My child, things that do not serve the evolution of the universe will not stand the test of time."

Be What You Wish Your World to *Become*

My child, this is Michael, your Universe Father. Train your minds to focus during these days of great change. The changes you wish to see within your planetary culture are those that you need to make within yourselves. Do you wish to see peace as a means of expression between people? Then train yourselves to focus on being peaceful, even during times of travail. Do you wish for people to be more loving towards one another? Then train yourselves to love your brothers and sisters, even if you do not understand them.

You see, my children, it is up to you to focus and train yourselves to *be* what you wish your planetary culture to *become*. It all begins with you, one person at a time. Your Mother and I will feed you with what you need, but you must first train yourselves to ask and then receive by focusing with all your heart, mind, and strength on what you wish to become.

My world will one day shine in *love*, *peace*, *mercy*, and *fairness*. But it will be accomplished by you, my awakened and enlivened children, who have made the ultimate commitment to become Godlike. Commit yourselves each day to this eventual outcome and know that you are making progress ever more faithfully moment by moment. Be in my peace!

Set an Intention for Each Day—and Each Moment

My child, this is your Father Michael. Each new day you greet is truly a new beginning. Your mind is receptive during this time, as it has not become fully engaged in your usual routine. Savor this time of arising each morning and spend a few moments setting your intention to follow the will of the Father Within. Doing so will enable a presence greater than yourself to participate in creating a joyful day full of growth-producing experiences.

One of the most significant lessons I learned as a human was to enter into each moment fully, and then appreciate what I was doing in that explicit moment. Setting the intention to be attuned to the leading of the Spirit helps you to dwell in each moment more mindfully. When you do so, you learn to listen to inner cues that tell you when to move on to the next activity. You find that your mind is not running off course into future projections or past memories. And this simplified mental approach lets you access a refreshing flow of love and light in each moment.

Train your minds in this manner, my child. Pay attention to how you are using this wonderful vehicle that connects you to your Mother and me and to your own Inner Spirit. We are here to lighten your human burdens, but it is up to *you* how you use your mental resources. Set the intention upon awakening to live in the flow of life, and observe how your day progresses!

> "One of the most significant lessons
> I learned as a human was to enter
> into each moment fully."

You Will Experience "Spiritual Growing Pains"

My child, this is your Father Michael. Sometimes in your growth process you will go through times that seem to be emotionally painful. But these moments could actually be helpful, for you may be experiencing spiritual "growing pains" that are expanding your minds into a better understanding of a hidden reality. This higher reality has been shielded from you for many eons of time, and as a result your bodies contain beliefs or emotional blockages that are resistant to it. Many of you are now in the process of shedding these blocks, so at times it will seem painful because you are letting go of something familiar.

However, what you are letting go of are erroneous beliefs that exist as thought-forms in your body. They represent false ideas of reality. You no longer need them, so it is time to tell them they cannot hold you back or hurt you anymore. When you encounter these painful thought-forms that stimulate negative feelings, come to your Mother and me. Ask us to expand you in our love and peace, so that you can relax your body and allow a higher energy-current to wash these thoughts and feelings out of you.

We love you, my child, and are pledged to help you move through these stages. You do not have to go it alone, nor should you, since we are the ones who can truly transform these old energies into something positive, useful, and life-regenerating in you. Come to us as often as you need. We want you to become the beautiful children of God that your souls long to express!

I Fully Understand the Human Experience

My child, this is Michael. When you look upon the situations of your world, remember that I am always with you. I will give you the courage and far-sightedness you need to go through this time of change with a hopeful heart. As the old crumbles away and a new awareness of a better world becomes more discernible in your hearts, know that it is *me* and *my presence* that are embracing your planet. Be glad and be appreciative for what is transpiring on our world!

Remember that I too had to walk through a vale of tears in order to find the Father's peace and love at the core of life. Because I drank deeply of the cup of human sorrow, I truly understand the fear and anxiety that is in the human heart. Remember also that I know how to guide you through these rough waters of change into the harbor of peace and safety. Come to me when you need my strength to carry you. You will receive it!

The more you embrace and allow for change, the easier it will be for what is transpiring to unfold. Look not to the destruction occurring in material form, but instead regard these events as opportunities to open many hearts to cooperation, sharing, compassion, and hope. In this way you will receive the upliftment you desire, plus whatever I may give you to augment your understanding and emotions. And when you experience this reassurance, my dear child, and share it with those in great need.

"Remember that I too had to walk through
a vale of tears in order to find the Father's
peace and love at the core of life."

Put on a Garment of Spiritual Luminosity

My children, this is Michael. Growing spiritually is sometimes likened to putting on a new garment of clothing. You are all accustomed to wearing certain colors and styles of clothes. Some people wear clothing to emulate a look that is considered fashionable. Others wear clothing that may appear shoddy or worn. Some people take pride in their clothes and use that as a mark of distinction or status.

Today I speak to you about *spiritual* clothing: putting on the garment of spiritual luminosity that shines from the inside out. This is customized raiment that no one else has—it is a unique manifestation of how your soul expresses itself to the world. It is quite exquisite and will always be attractive because you wear it with distinction and honor.

Spiritual clothing is different than physical clothing because it will never tear or wear out. It has a resilience and texture that depicts the best in you. Since it is customized, you can be identified by what you "wear" when you are engaged with your brethren. Think about this garment today, my beloved, as you wear your spiritual clothes while you go about your daily activities. Let them speak to those you meet, and observe how the clothing of Spirit affects the world around you.

Trouble Not Others for Your Validation

My child, this is Michael, your Father in Spirit. Children have a way of bickering and jockeying for position, approval, and recognition. But my children who feel my love, and know it deeply in their souls, need not concern themselves with such attitudes and activities. They already feel my love and know my peace of mind that secures their place in our family. Your brothers and sisters will all benefit from your calm awareness of your settled place in our home.

Therefore, become aware of those times when you want to put yourself in a position of recognition and approval by others. Instead, switch your awareness to *me*. I will validate you in a way that suits you, so that you need not trouble your fellows for their recommendation. They may not be in a position to give it to you anyway, and desiring it from them can only lead to disappointment.

Instead, recognize your true need, and realize that there is no requirement of yours that I cannot fulfill or adjust. If you have a need that seems to be ego-centered, and if it is showing itself as a longing, then bring it to me that I may help you outgrow its childish hold on your self-concept and awareness. Think not that any need is too insignificant or petty to bring to me. I will help you with all your desires and issues and align them in the ways of rightful thinking and balanced feeling. Be in my peace!

"Think not that any need is too
insignificant or petty to bring to me."

Receive My Vibrations of Truth, Light, and Liberty

Beloved child, this is your Father Michael who holds you tenderly in my heart. Even though you are situated a long way from your true home at the center of my universe, we are connected always through the Spirit of Truth that rings in your heart. Now, more than ever before, your heart wants my vibrations of truth, light, and liberty to ring through your body.

A strong undercurrent of Spirit runs through your energy system. This current is causing a disruption of the old patterns of understanding that have long set back this planet from its evolution towards the higher culture of Light and Life. Allow this energy to become stronger in your hearts, my beloved. Trust that this is *me* running through your system, cutting away the dead beliefs and paradigms that have fostered your feelings of unworthiness and shame. Remember, you are divine sons and daughters of the living Creator and you have a natural nobility that no one can ever take from you.

Rest in your Mother and breathe in these words: *truth*, *light*, and *liberty*. Allow them to circulate through your mind; feel how much you want their language to live inside you. Give me permission to cut away the brambles of old ideas you are still attached to, and allow your body to release its tension through breathing deeply and mindfully. You are safe in my hands as you are restored and renewed in the light of my love that liberates you from the past and reveals the truth of who you really are.

> "A strong undercurrent of Spirit
> runs through your energy system."

Your Heart is a Mighty Force for Goodness, Truth, and Beauty

My child, this is Michael, your Universe Father. What makes your heart happy? Think about this for a few moments and also reflect upon it in your heart. This vital sensing part of your being is not just a physical organ; it is also able to receive spiritual energy and then translate it into an energy that feeds your body. As you think about what makes your heart happy, notice what changes within your body.

Your true power is within your heart, more than you may be aware at this point in time. Within this wonderful sensing portal is a mighty force for goodness, truth, and beauty. Allow your mind to settle into what makes your heart happy. To do this, open your creative imagination and allow your ideas to soar into the realm of the divine—the realm where perfection and ideals live. Attach your desires to this realm, my child, and allow your heart to feed upon divinity. Notice how your body responds as you engage your thoughts in this activity.

As part of this process, I ask you to also discern the power of your thoughts. Appreciate that you have the capacity to change your thinking at any point in time. When you notice that you have gravitated into fear or doubt, simply *change your mind*. Practice these good mental habits, especially while focusing on what makes your heart happy, and feed yourself upon the goodness that comes from your Divine Sources.

"Open your creative imagination and allow
your ideas to soar into the realm of the divine."

With My Help, Discern the Truth in Your Heart

My child, this is your Father Michael. The energy of the Spirit of Truth is rising in the hearts of my children of this world. This circuit is the connecting link from me to you, and it serves as that presence within you that resonates when you experience *truth*. This sensibility is a powerful indicator that can serve you when confronted with complex information from your outer world.

Become familiar with how to use this presence within. Simply focus on your heart and ask for clarification: "Father, I just heard something important. Please help me to discern if this is true." Stay focused in your heart, that place of desire for what you need to know, and I will speak to you. If you listen, you will glean more awareness of what is true; this will especially be so when you let go of what you *think* the answer might be and allow what *is* true to come into your mind. This method will take practice, as the intellect tends to be proud of what it knows and doesn't surrender easily.

You, however, *are* in control of your thoughts. You can decide to shift your focus of awareness from your head to your heart where the Spirit of Truth can speak to you. Practice, practice, practice, my child, to become a master at this, and your delight and joy will augment as you increasingly learn to trust in this wonderful connection between us.

Never will I fail you; you can only gain by trusting in this connecting link between us and allowing it to grow stronger through your continued practice of turning to me. Use your mind wisely, my children, and remember it is in your *heart* that all of your answers lie!

Rise to the Occasions Your Angels Put Before You

My child, this is Michael—your Universe Father. Growing a hardy soul capable of making the long journey to Paradise perfection requires that you have many experiences to draw out the best in you—experiences that allow you to manifest your potential of personality gifts that come from the Father at the center of all life. Why bemoan your earthly existence when you have so many opportunities to choose what is right, good, true, and beautiful? You too often allow yourselves to be dominated by base emotions that deter the Spirit from having access to your minds, besmirching your beautiful souls with feelings that are unworthy of sons and daughters of God.

Rise above your emotions, my child, and seek the best in who you are! After all, there is greatness in all of you—yes, it is untapped potential—but you alone have the joy and the thrill of *bringing it to life*. Seek out new challenges with gusto and vigor that will empower your Spirit to guide you through to victory. The time is now, and you will have many more opportunities to rise to the occasions your angels put before you. Know that your brothers and sisters will be catalyzed by your goodness and rightful action.

I will accompany you through these occasions of your life. I will give you my mind when your own mind and understanding falter. Look for the greatness within you, my child, and commit to bringing your beauty to a world awakening to the glory of Spirit!

Liberate Others by Speaking the Truth

My beloved child, this is your Father Michael. Truth is that liberating quality of information that your heart perceives when your desire is turned Godward. People may say that they "speak their truth," but what they really do is speak their feelings and beliefs. Speaking *truth* is different. It creates a resonance that the heart perceives, even if it is just a slight recognition.

So in "speaking your truth" remember that your motivation and intention are of utmost importance. People will take notice when you are really *speaking truth* rather than simply describing something you have a certain degree of understanding or feel strongly about. In speaking *this* truth, you are representing me to others. You are sharing a spiritual dimension that they need, and they will feel it at some level. While you do not always know what is true, when you open your hearts to me I will share my thoughts with you and feed you with a quality of living truth that, in sharing, will benefit both the speaker and the listener.

Remember that your brothers and sisters are now hungry for truth. Open your heart to them and their needs. Feed them well by asking me to respond to them. Center yourself in your heart and then speak what you perceive to be coming forth from your thoughts. Practice and take time to master this, my children, and you will find that through your speaking *truth*, many ears will now hear!

> "In speaking the truth, you are
> representing me to others."

The "Baby" You Are Birthing Is a New World

Beloved child, this is your Father Michael. Move into your Spirit, my child, into your center, into your heart. Now is the time to shift from your old understanding of your world to the hope that is swelling in your heart for a better future. This hope is a catalyzing power to stimulate you into action. The action I ask you to perform is to center yourself within and to gain confidence in my presence growing within you. This presence will endow you with power and perseverance, and give you the stamina you need to birth a new world.

Think of what you are going through as "hard labor"; the baby you are birthing is a new world and a new self-awareness. The contractions squeeze you tightly as you move through the canal of change and transformation. Trust that your Mother is guiding you safely into a new dimension; trust that my hands are there to catch you as you emerge from the birth canal. Trust that my hands are holding your world safely as it emerges into the light of the universe. Trust what is happening around you and let go . . . let go . . . let go.

You have lived so long under tight control that you find it hard to let go into Spirit. Trust is the food your soul needs to open and allow that which is new to guide you. Trust us, trust the energies around you, trust yourself. Trust the universe, and watch what goodness comes out of chaos.

You Have an Eternity of Time in Which to Grow

My beloved, this is Michael. Time is a commodity you have in plenitude. You all lead busy lives that are sometimes in service to a clock. But when it comes to your spiritual growth, you have an eternity of time in which to grow. You do not become Spirit all at once; instead, you can expect your unfolding to be a slow process that will allow you to savor the journey—one experience at a time.

It is the attitude of gratefulness that conditions your enjoyment of what you experience. Even the most arduous of challenges can turn into your biggest asset and blessing by instead regarding it as a great learning tool to add to your life skills. Learn to slow down to appreciate what is in front of you in the moment. It becomes easier to enjoy and appreciate life when you take it at its natural rhythm instead of squeezing in as many activities as you think you must do—trying to get so many things done in time!

Learn how to use time to your spiritual advantage, my children. The passing of time is the foundational structure of your evolutionary nature, and you can become masters of time with the right attitude toward it each day. Slow down, do not hurry; know that all is well. By re-pacing your life you will perceive a richness in time that will provide you with many more benefits, once you truly master its ways and cadence. Trust in the power of time and learn what it truly wants to teach you!

Learn What It Means to be a Universe Citizen

Beloved child, this is your Father Michael. There is so much for you to explore as you open your heart to your Mother and me and to your universe brothers and sisters. As valuable members of our universe family, you are coming into a greater awareness of your role and the privileges and responsibilities you have. Always take time each day to spend with your Mother and me in the quiet of your heart, that we may guide you into feeling more a part of our family. Come home to your heart!

Exploration of the universe is a journey you will increasingly enjoy as your heart opens. What is there to learn? Everything you have desired to understand! What is there to experience? Everything your heart has desired! This is not the same kind of experience you encounter in your material life; in your afterlife of the eternal career to come, you can enjoy life in the universe by always expanding your desires to learn and grow and master the lessons that make you good universe citizens and noble human beings.

With our guidance we will help you achieve these things, my child. We will feed your minds and hearts with what you need to master the lessons you experience in your daily lives. From the inside out you will learn what it is to be universe citizens. Then go on to help your human brothers and sisters experience the love you know so well in your souls.

"Master the lessons that make you good
universe citizens and noble human beings."

You Will Be Educated in the Ways of the Universe

My children, this is Michael. As your Universe Father, it is my responsibility to take care of my children—to help them mature into noble universe citizens ready to take on the exploration and administration of the universe. This is *an undertaking of eternity*, and you are given the choice of whether or not to participate in this grand adventure. Because you must be educated as to what this means, you will be introduced to higher cosmic philosophies and their implications. You have a right to be educated into the ways of the universe.

For many eons of time, humanity has been influenced by a culture that tried to improve upon the divine plan. What has been created in *perfection* cannot be altered except by the One in whom the creation ensued. Those that tried to build this planetary culture have erred by ignoring the laws of the universe, and humanity has been struggling ever since to free itself from these aberrations. Now, my children, my plan of correction is fully in place. Now, the doors of heaven have opened to teach you what you need to know.

Come into the stillness of your heart, the quiet of your mind, and ask for the lessons of universe operation to be imprinted upon your mind. Your Mother and I will share with you what you need to know and experience. You have a right to your divine birthright, and we are delighted to help you regain it—much to your delight as well!

"Now, my children, my plan
of correction is fully in place."

About the Center for Christ Consciousness

The Center for Christ Consciousness is dedicated to helping people develop their personal relationship with Spirit, especially with our Divine Parents and with the Spirit of God that indwells each of us. We offer a variety of services and materials to enhance your spiritual growth and facilitate healing on all levels.

Private sessions by phone, in person, or on Skype with Donna D'Ingillo: Experience what it means to be re-parented in God's loving embrace, and to build the foundation of a new self-concept based on intimacy with your Divine Parents and your Indwelling Spirit of God. These sessions augment your ability to feel valued, worthy, and more connected to your life purpose. They also bring in new spiritual energies that are designed to foster the development of higher consciousness, and that can even touch your DNA strands as your Spiritual Parents heal traumatic memory patterns.

Workshops, conferences, and seminars: Benefit from a wealth of information on spiritual growth, healing, and soul transformation by participating in real-time online group sessions via our website, in phone conference line sessions, or in-person gatherings. I can also design sessions to meet your group's specific needs.

Instruction in the practice of Stillness: Learn how to quiet the mind in order to discern divine presences and communicate with them.

Books and CDs: Read and hear the teachings of our Divine Parents and open your heart to their messages through these specially designed materials:

- *Teach Us to Love* is the manual for developing your relationship with your Indwelling Spirit of God. The companion audio recording, *Come into the Stillness*, is highly recommended for training your mind to listen for the divine Inner Voice in a meditative experience. (See next page for details.)

- *Experiencing Your Divine Parents,* the audio recording companion to *Divine Mother, Divine Father,* will foster your experiences with our Spirit Mother and Father, so that you may feel their love and their validation of who you are as a child of God.

Further teachings from our Divine Mother and Father are available by *Joining our Family* on our website, as well as video and audio presentations that provide insight and support in daily life situations and contain meditative experiences to support your spiritual development. More information can be found under the Living Christ Consciousness page: Experiencing God.

The CCC provides a place of peace, receptivity, and acceptance. May you find it to be a welcoming home and support for your journey towards enlightenment and fulfillment.

For further information on all our offerings, visit our CCC website at:
www.centerforchristconsciousness.org

Teach Us to Love: Finding Unconditional Love through Communion with God

This unique book is presented by celestial ministers who are profound teachers to humankind. They offer instruction emphasizing communicating with God, that is, how to quiet your mind and experience God, who is the source of your loving Inner Spirit. This sublime experience of divine love validates you as a person and is the key to loving others and finding happiness with life. Through this inner exploration you will discover ways to overcome emotional wounds, enhance your spiritual growth, and become more loving of yourself and others.

While the messages of *Divine Mother, Divine Father* provide the foundation to perceive yourself as a son and daughter in our loving universe family, *Teach Us to Love* emphasizes the practice of quieting the mind to perceive your own indwelling Spirit that offers you direct and highly personal divine guidance. Developing intimacy with your inner Spirit provides the opportunity to allow Godly thoughts and emotions to uplift your thinking and feeling into the realms of peace and joy. Your Spirit functions in concert with your Divine Parents to provide the inner structure of spiritual support that allows you may grow and prosper as a worthy child of the universe.

You can access your inner Spirit's voice through the practice of "stillness," and this is especially facilitated through the consciousness-raising technique called the *Seven Steps of Stillness* that is provided in *Teach Us to Love.* You will also learn facets of effective prayer, forgiveness as a spiritual healing tool, how to discern the presence of God in others, and fascinating lessons about living in faith and healing all levels of your life.

Stimulating and thought-provoking, *Teach Us to Love* will augment your insight into your real life —your spiritual life.

The companion audio recording, *Come into the Stillness,* provides a helpful structure (the Seven Steps of Stillness) to train the mind to move beyond incessant mental chatter that you may perceive the divine inner voice. This raises your consciousness to the higher realms where your indwelling Spirit is able to communicate the answers to your life's pressing challenges that you may increasingly perceive your reality through God's eyes.

To order these materials see the *About the Center for Christ Consciousness* page.

An Overview of *The Urantia Book*

The Urantia Book is a 2,097-page tome that claims to be an epochal divine revelation to our planet, and is a unique artifact in the history of religion. Some regard the Urantia Revelation as a postmodern Bible, and since its publication in 1955, the book has sold over a million copies in English in all versions (and more than 200,000 in Spanish), and has been translated into 17 languages. Here is an overview look at the anatomy of *The Urantia Book*, which contains 196 papers and is divided into four sections:

Part I. The Central and Superuniverses presents the infinitely loving and merciful nature of the Universal Father, the Eternal Son, and the Infinite Spirit. It depicts the nature and activities of this Eternal Trinity and other high universe personalities, while offering many other revelations about the ultimate nature of deity, divinity, and the universe of universes. Part I also describes the extent and structure of the far-flung cosmic domains of physical creation, in particular painting a thrilling picture of a perfect, eternal central universe that lies at the cosmic center of an evolving time-space universe comprised of outlying galaxy clusters containing trillions of inhabited planets—and much more. The lofty exposition of cosmic realities provided in Part I is considered by most Urantians (i.e., Urantia "reader-believers") to be pure revelation.

Part II. The Local Universe details the nature and structure of the "local" sector of our Milky Way galaxy that contains nearly four million inhabited planets. This account covers the physical constitution of the local universe, its administration and history going back to its first appearance over 400 billion years ago, and details its vast celestial host. It offers considerable detail about life after death and the plan for eternal ascent for those who survive death. (Most people from Urantia will awake after death on what is known as the "first mansion world"— the first heavenly abode. They begin their afterlife career there, undergoing a vast regime of spiritual training, holistic education, and cosmic socialization whose description comprises many sections spread across Parts I–III in the text.) One of the highlights of Part II is the introduction of the "master sovereign" and Creator of our local universe, known as Christ Michael. It is he who incarnated as Jesus of Nazareth on Urantia. Also introduced is Michael's complemental deity partner and coequal Creator with him of this local universe, known as the Universe Mother Spirit, and her vast and varied orders of ministering angels. It is these two beings who grace us with the teachings in this book.

Part III. The History of Urantia narrates the origin of our solar system and offers a chronological account of the history of Earth ("Urantia") and the evolution of all life on the planet, including an anthropological, sociological, racial, and spiritual history of humankind. This section also presents for the first time the story of the four previous epochal revelations to Urantia—with the Urantia Revelation being the fifth. Significantly, Part III includes detail about the so-called Lucifer Rebellion that traumatized Urantia and 36 other planets in the local system in the far-distant past. Lucifer was the angelic-administrative head of our local system of 1,000 inhabited planets, and most of our own planet's angelic administration joined in rebellion with him and his chief lieutenant, Satan. The disaster of planet-wide rebellion led to the default of the first two phases of epochal revelation on our sphere, including the Earth mission of Adam and Eve, one of the most dramatic and fascinating narratives in the Urantia text. And this gloomy start to humankind's history was a key reason why Christ Michael chose to incarnate on our lowly sphere; Urantia's disastrous history offered the starkest backdrop against which to demonstrate Michael's sublime and merciful love for his most wayward creatures. Part III also provides a comprehensive picture of the nature of personal spiritual growth, including soul evolution before and after death; the true nature and function of religion; and the concept of the indwelling spirit, or "thought adjuster"—the God-fragment that comes to live within the mind of each of us at the moment when our first moral decision is made as a child. Finally, and equally as important, Part III also reveals the "finite" and evolving aspect of deity, known as the Supreme Being. It should be noted that many human sources are woven throughout the revelatory material in this part of the text, which the revelators indicate to be the case as one feature of the cocreative technique of revelation.

Part IV. The Life and Teachings of Jesus contains a lengthy account of Jesus' life that is based, we are told, on the angelic record of his days on Earth; it in fact presents the world's most detailed biography of Jesus. This powerful narrative often covers events day by day and sometimes even hour by hour—including the story of the so-called "lost years" of Jesus's childhood, adolescence, and young adulthood. It also contains an extensive and detailed account of his private and public ministries and his death and resurrection, and closes with the story of his bestowal of his Spirit of Truth at Pentecost. Perhaps the most remarkable material in Part IV is its culminating paper, "The Faith of Jesus." (The book's 196 chapters are known as "papers.") This paper's superb "summa" of Jesus's life and message has long been the supreme inspiration for thousands of people worldwide. Ultimately, readers of Part VI will be able to replace their image of the somewhat mythic Jesus of the Bible—who sacrificed his life for our sins—with an updated Jesus who teaches a gospel of loving service, self-respect, soul evolution, artistic living, and self-mastery in the context of planetary and cosmic citizenship.

Glossary

adjudication; adjudication of Lucifer Rebellion
The case of *Gabriel vs. Lucifer* was launched early in the twentieth century before the courts of the Ancients of Days (see entry), concurrently with the reception of the Papers in Chicago that would later become *The Urantia Book*. Gabriel vs. Lucifer was fully adjudicated in the fall of 1985, after which Christ Michael launched the Correcting Time and later the Teaching Mission on our planet. The Adjudication meant that the quarantine of Urantia could be lifted so that all "off-world" communication circuits to the planet could be reinstated. The reasons for the Rebellion and the story of its aftermath are discussed at length in *The Urantia Book* and especially in Papers 52 and 53.

adjutant mind-spirits; seven adjutant mind-spirits; adjutants of wisdom and worship
Adjutants represent the functioning of the "mind ministry" of the Infinite Spirit (see entry), and are of origin in the Mother Spirit of any local universe. Adjutant mind-spirits are not beings or entities, but operate more like connectivity circuits as they operate with the creature mind. The first five adjutants—the spirits of intuition, understanding, courage, knowledge, and counsel—minister to the lower levels of experiential minds (animals and humans), and the last two—the spirits of worship and wisdom—operate only in mortal minds with spiritual potential. Adjutant mind-spirits have been compared to the "seven chakras" system in Vedanta and other teachings about the human energy body. [See UB, Paper 36, sec. 5.]

Christ Michael; Michael; Creator Son; Jesus Christ
Michael is our local universe father, creator, and sovereign, and is also known to us as Jesus Christ, who incarnated as Jesus of Nazareth on our planet. He is of the order of Michael—high beings with creator prerogatives who are also known as Creator Sons; they are directly

of origin from God the Father and God the Son. In partnership with the Mother Spirits who are their equals (see "Mother Spirit"), Michaels create local universes and their myriad inhabitants, over which they rule with love and mercy. Their unending love for us is typified in the fact that they may incarnate in the likeness of their creatures on the worlds they have created.

central universe; Havona; billion worlds
Havona, the central universe, is not a time creation; it is an eternal existence. This never-beginning, never-ending universe consists of one billion spheres of sublime perfection. At the center of Havona is the stationary and absolutely stabilized Isle of Paradise (see "Paradise"). The mass of this central creation is far in excess of the total known mass of all seven sectors of the grand universe (the time-space creations).

Correcting Time
This is an umbrella term used by our celestial teachers for the current period of celestially inspired transformations occurring throughout the planet. The Correcting Time is a much vaster project than the Teaching Mission (see entry). The Teaching Mission is characterized by its explicit use of the Urantia Revelation as a reference; the Correcting Time does not. The common element of the Correcting Time in all its features is a dramatic increase in celestial assistance for the purpose of fostering planetary evolution, both secular and spiritual. Technically speaking, the possibility for such celestial intervention had to await the reconnection of certain "spiritual circuits" made possible by the lifting of the quarantine (see entry) that was placed on our planet because of its early involvement in the Lucifer Rebellion (see entry).

Eternal Son
The Eternal Son is the great mercy minister to all creation. As the second person of the divine Trinity, he is known as the Original Son, and along with God the Father, he is the cocreator of other divine sons. He is the source of spirit, the administrator of all spirit, and the center of spirit in the universe and therefore all things spiritual are drawn to him; he is co-eternal and co-ordinate with the Father, and is a full equal to the Father. "The Eternal Son is the perfect and final expression of the 'first' personal and absolute concept of the Universal Father. Accordingly, whenever and however the Father personally and absolutely expresses himself,

he does so through his Eternal Son, who ever has been, now is and ever will be, the living and divine Word. The Eternal Son is the spiritual personalization of the Father's universal and infinite concept of divine reality, unqualified spirit, and absolute personality. As the Father is the First Great Source and Center, so the Eternal Son is the Second Great Source and Center." [See UB: Papers 6 and 7.]

God the Father; God; Father; Paradise Father
God is love; as the universal Father, God is the first person of deity, the First Source and Center of all things and beings. According to the Urantia Revelation, the term "God" always denotes personality. God the Father is the infinite and eternal God of love, as well as Creator, Controller, and Upholder of the universe of all universes. The first person of deity—God the Father—loves us with an attitude analogous to that of a divine father; the love and mercy of God the Son, the second person of deity, can be considered akin to the love of a mother. God the Spirit is the third person of deity, also known as the Infinite Spirit.

Holy Spirit—see Mother Spirit

indwelling spirit; God within; Father Fragment; Thought Adjuster
The phrase indwelling spirit or "God-within" refers to an actual fragment of God the Father that indwells every normal-minded and morally conscious human being. This spark of God is wholly subservient to our will, yet represents the actual will of God, resident in our own minds. Through the practice of stillness, meditative worship, and loving service to others, we can attune ourselves to the influence of this inner divinity, thereby discerning the will of God for us as individuals. Also known as the Father Fragment or Mystery Monitor, the indwelling spirit is God's gift to each of us in addition to our personality, and its influence arouses our hunger for perfection and our quest for the divine. In addition, our "spark of God" and our material mind, working together, actually create our soul (see "soul"). According to *The Urantia Book*, the great goal of our spiritual evolution is to actually *fuse* with the indwelling spirit—i.e., come into complete union and identification with the indwelling spirit of God, and by so doing achieve immortality.

Light and Life; Age of Light and Life
The goal of all inhabited planets, the final evolutionary attainment of any world of time and space, is known as the Age of Light and Life. When a world has reached this utopian state of evolutionary consummation, its achievements along the way will have included the attainment of one worldwide language, one blended race, one unified world religion, universal peace, and a very advanced state of prosperity and happiness

local system
A local system consists of about one thousand inhabited or inhabitable worlds. Cold worlds or planets too near their suns, and other spheres not suitable for creature habitation, are not included in this group. One thousand local worlds adapted to support life are called a system, but in the younger systems only a comparatively small number of these worlds may be inhabited. Each inhabited planet is presided over by a Planetary Prince, and each local system has an architectural sphere as its headquarters and is ruled by a System Sovereign. Our local system, named *Satania*, is not yet complete. So far there are 619 inhabited planets in the system, and there will be one thousand when it is complete. Urantia was the 606th world to have life implanted on it within the system. The administrative head of Satania is a *Lanonandek Son* named *Lanaforge*. He has served since shortly after Lucifer, the previous administrative head, was deposed and incarcerated for disloyalty to the universe government. [See UB, Papers 45 and 46.]

local universe; Nebadon
Our local universe, called *Nebadon*, was created by Christ Michael, and is ruled by Michael as Master Son and Sovereign, and by Nebadonia, our Mother Spirit or Divine Minister. The local universe administrative headquarters is *Salvington*, which is also the abode of Michael and Nebadonia. Nebadon is still in the process of formation and will eventually contain 10,000,000 inhabited planets. Nebadon is one of 700,000 local universes within the Grand Universe. [See UB, Papers 32 and 33.] In Urantia Book cosmology, Paradise is a stationary body at the center of the space-time universe (see "central universe" and "Paradise"), which is surrounded by a central universe of inherently perfect worlds, which is in turn encircled by seven discrete aggregations of galaxies (galaxy clusters) called *superuniverses*. Each superuniverse is comprised of 700,000 local universes. As stated, *The Urantia Book* indicates that a local universe is made

up of approximately 10,000,000 inhabitable planets and is evolving toward perfection. Each local universe is ruled by one of the Creator Sons of God of the order of Michael.

Lucifer; Lucifer Rebellion
Lucifer was a high celestial being and brilliant administrator of a system of 607 inhabited planets, who with his first assistant *Satan* launched a rebellion against the local universe government of Christ Michael some 200,000 years ago. Lucifer's insurrection created pandemonium in the celestial hierarchy and on our planet—as well as in 36 other planets in our local system. Among other contentions, Lucifer claimed that the Universal Father does not really exist, and he attacked the right of Christ Michael to assume sovereignty of Nebadon in the name of the Father. The majority of celestial beings in the celestial hierarchy of our planet went over to the way of Lucifer, causing major distortions and aberrations ever since in the evolution and history of our planet. The planetwide era of conscious awakening known as the Correcting Time (of which the Teaching Mission is a part), was launched in the mid-1980s, we are told, after the final adjudication of the Lucifer rebellion in celestial courts.

Michael—see Christ Michael

Michael Sons; order of Michael
This order of Paradise Son, some 700,000 in number in the universe, are created by the Universal Father and the Eternal Son. Each are known as the "only-begotten Son" because, even though they function alike in their domains, each has an individual personality that makes him unlike any other Michael Son. These Sons are the personification of the Paradise Father-Son, to and in their local universes. Each is destined to create a local universe of his own making, and with the Mother Spirit, to create the living beings that will inhabit this physical creation. Each Michael must earn the right to govern his local universe creation as its sovereign, by completing seven bestowals, in which he incarnates as one of each order of beings that he himself created. In this way he becomes a wise, merciful and loving brother and Father to his sons and daughters. [See UB, Papers 21 and 33.]

Michael; Christ Michael
The creator of our local universe, Christ Michael, is Father and brother to all living beings of his creation, and is one and the same as Jesus Christ, who incarnated on Earth. He possesses

and represents all the divine attributes and powers of the Eternal Son within the local universe of Nebadon, and has additional power and authority to fully represent the Universal Father to his creatures. To our local universe, Michael represents God; he is omnipotent, omniscient, and omnipresent. He is ably assisted by his consort, the Universe Mother Spirit, known as *Nebadonia.* His main concerns within his realm are creation, sustenance, and ministry. He does not participate in judicial affairs, as creators never sit in judgment on their creatures. [See UB, Paper 33.]

Mother Spirit; Universe Mother Spirit; Nebadonia; the Holy Spirit

Just as Michael is our local universe Father, the Mother Spirit is our local universe Mother. As Christ Michael is a personalization of the first and second persons of the Trinity, the Creative Mother Spirit is a personalization of the third person of deity. She is Christ Michael's consort in the administration and in the ministry of love and mercy to the myriad of planets in *Nebadon* (see entry). Among the many powers and duties of Mother Spirit is her ability to give life; she supplies the essential factor of living plasm to all creatures high and low. She also provides the universal "womb of consciousness" in which we live. This endowment of consciousness affords us the capacity to think, feel, and act—all made possible by the vehicle of her seven *adjutant mind-spirits* (see entry). She also loves and ministers to us through her vast retinue of angels and other ministering celestial beings.

Nebadon; local universe

This is the name of the local universe in which our planet is located. Nebadon presently contains approximately 3,800,000 inhabited planets. It is a relatively young universe and sits on the outer edges of *Orvonton,* the superuniverse in which it is located. Nebadon is ruled by Christ Michael, also known as Jesus Christ, and his consort, the Mother Spirit, who are the creators of Nebadon.

Paradise

At the literal center of the cosmos, yet outside of space and time, is the only stationary body in all creation, and the Urantia revelation designates this reality as Paradise. God is personally present on Paradise, and from his infinite being flow the floodstreams of life, energy, and personality to all universe. Paradise is a stupendously large island located at the geographical center of infinity. All physical energy and all cosmic-force circuits, including all forms of gravity, have their origin at Paradise. It also has residential zones; all God-conscious mortal will someday attain and reside on Paradise.

personality
Personality is that part of a person by which we know them as unique, and designates those personal qualities that endure and which are recognizable regardless of changes in age, status, behavior or other external qualities. We are told that personality is a high and divine gift to each person from God the Father. It is that changeless metaphysical quality that confers upon them their unique identity in the cosmos, and could be called the "image of God" within us. Personality is absolutely unique and immutable; it does not in itself evolve, but its relationship with the indwelling spirit (Thought Adjuster) and the soul continually evolves. Functionally, personality also acts as the unifier and integrator of all aspects of an individual's relationship with his or her environment.

Planetary Prince
A Planetary Prince appears on a world when it has for the first time evolved primitive human beings of will status. Although a Planetary Prince is invisible to the humans, his staff is not. The staff sets up schools and teach a variety of skills, such as basic cultivation of the soil, home building, and spiritual culture. The classes are progressive in nature; the mortals are taught agriculture, food preservation, government, sanitation, pottery, metal working and so on. The students are then sent out among their people to share the knowledge. The Prince and his staff normally stay on a world, teaching ever-higher concepts of wisdom, philosophy, brotherhood and religion, until a planet reaches the Age of Light and Life. Urantia's Prince *Caligastia* served admirably for 300,000 years before following his superior, Lucifer, into rebellion, about 200,000 years ago. Caligastia was then removed from his post. (See Lucifer Rebellion.)

quarantine; quarantined worlds
After a period of observation, worlds and systems that have participated in open rebellion or disloyalty to the Creator Son are placed in isolation until the courts of the Ancients of Days (see entry) are able to rule on the matter. Urantia and 36 other inhabited worlds were placed in quarantine (all communications severed) when Lucifer and Caligastia went into rebellion against the universe government. The isolation continued for 200,000 years, until

the adjudication took place in 1985. Our world is now being normalized and brought back into the communication circuits through the action of Michael's Correcting Time.

soul
The indwelling spirit or Thought Adjuster is a perfect gift of God, but the soul is an experiential achievement. As we choose the divine will in our lives, the effect of this experience is that our soul grows in substance and quality. We are told in *The Urantia Book* that the indwelling spirit is the *father* of our soul, just as the material mind—as a result of its moral choice—is the *mother* of the emerging soul. In the afterlife, it is the soul alone that survives death and becomes the container of our actual identity, through the agency of our personality.

Spirit of Truth
This is the unique spiritual endowment conferred on each person on this planet from our Creator Son, Christ Michael. This high and pure spiritual influence was first gifted universally to humankind on the day of Pentecost, just after Jesus' resurrection. The Spirit of Truth enhances each person's ability to recognize truth. Its effectiveness is limited by each person's free-will consecration of his or her will to doing the will of God, but its influence is universal. When actively sought, the Spirit of Truth purifies the human heart and leads the individual to formulate a life purpose based on the love of truth.

Trinity; Paradise Trinity
This refers to the eternal deity union of the Universal Father, the Eternal Son, and the Infinite Spirit.

Urantia ("you-ran-sha")
Urantia is the name by which our planet is known in our local universe, according to the celestial authors of *The Urantia Book*. Urantia is said to be a disturbed planet by virtue of its participation in the Lucifer Rebellion, and yet is a blessed planet because it was the site of the incarnation bestowal of Michael, as Jesus of Nazareth.